**TEACHER'S PET PUBLICATIONS**

LITPLAN TEACHER PACK
for
Monster

based on the book by
Walter Dean Myers

Written by
Mary B. Collins

© 2006 Teacher's Pet Publications
All Rights Reserved

This **LitPlan** for *Monster*
has been brought to you by Teacher's Pet Publications, Inc.

Copyright Teacher's Pet Publications 2006

Only the student materials in this unit plan (such as worksheets, study questions, and tests) may be reproduced multiple times for use in the purchaser's classroom.

For any additional copyright questions,
contact Teacher's Pet Publications.

www.tpet.com

TABLE OF CONTENTS - *Monster*

Introduction	5
Unit Objectives	7
Reading Assignment Sheet	8
Unit Outline	9
Study Questions (Short Answer)	13
Quiz/Study Questions (Multiple Choice)	24
Pre-reading Vocabulary Worksheets	45
Lesson One (Introductory Lesson)	63
Writing Assignment 1	71
Oral Reading Evaluation Form	76
Writing Assignment 2	81
Writing Evaluation Form	82
Extra Writing Assignments/Discussion ?s	84
Nonfiction Assignment Sheet	89
Writing Assignment 3	91
Vocabulary Review Activities	92
Unit Review Activities	93
Unit Tests	97
Unit Resource Materials	137
Vocabulary Resource Materials	157

A FEW NOTES ABOUT THE AUTHOR
WALTER DEAN MYERS

MYERS, WALTER DEAN , 1937- Born Walter Milton Myers, in Martinsburg, West Virginia, his mother died when he was three. He was then adopted and raised by Florence and Herbert Dean. The Deans moved to Harlem shortly after. In *Something About the Author*, Volume 71, Myers said he "lived in an exciting corner of the renowned Black capital and in an exciting era. The people I met there, the things I did, have left a permanent impression on me."

Myers began reading at age four, and started writing when he was ten. Since his parents did not consider writing as a career possibility, he was not encouraged to write. He enlisted in the U. S. Army when he was seventeen, and served for three years. During that time he continued to read and write for pleasure. He attended City College of the City University of New York, and received a B. A. degree from Empire State College in 1984.

Winning a writing contest sponsored by the Council on Interracial Books for Children in the late 1960's changed his life. The winning entry, a picture book titled *Where Did the Day Go?*, was published in 1969. Myers continued writing after that. Most of his books center on Black teens growing up in an urban environment. In addition, Myers has written science fiction, non-fiction, mysteries, and adventure stories.

Awards include the ALA notable book citation in 1975 for *Fast Sam, Cool Clyde, and Stuff*, 1978 for *It Ain't All For Nothin'*, 1979 for *The Young Landlords*, and 1988 for *Me, Mop, and the Moondance Kid* and *Scorpions*. He also received several ALA Best Books for Young Adults citations, including 1988 for *Scorpions* and *Fallen Angels*. He received the Coretta Scott King Award for fiction in 1980 for *The Young Landlords*, in 1985 for *Motown and Didi*, and 1988 for *Fallen Angels*. *Scorpions* was a Newbery Honor Book in 1989. His most recent book, *Slam!*, has won the Coretta Scott King Award, and was named the ALA Best Book for Young Adults . Myers continues to live and write from his home in New Jersey.

Published Works

Where Does the Day Go? 1969
The Dragon Takes a Wife, 1972
The Dancers, 1972.
Fly, Jimmy, Fly!, 1974
Fast Sam, Cool Clyde, and Stuff, 1975
Brainstorm, 1977
Mojo and the Russians, 1977
Victory for Jamie, 1977
It Ain't All for Nothin', 1978
The Young Landlords, 1979
The Golden Serpent, 1980
The Black Pearl and the Ghost, 1980
Hoops, 1981
The Legend of Tarik, 1981
Won't Know Till I Get There, 1982

The Nicholas Factor, 1983
Tales of a Dead King, 1983
Motown and Didi: A Love Story, 1984
The Outside Shot, 1984
Sweet Illusions, 1986
Crystal, 1987
Scorpions, 1988
Me, Mop, and the Moondance Kid, 1988
Fallen Angels, 1988
The Mouse Rap, 1990
Somewhere in the Darkness, 1992
Mop, Moondance, and the Nagasaki Knights, 1992
The Righteous Revenge of Artemis Bonner, 1992
Slam! 1996

INTRODUCTION *Monster*

This unit has been designed to develop students' reading, writing, thinking, and language skills through exercises and activities related to *Monster* by Walter Dean Myers. It includes eighteen lessons, supported by extra resource materials.

In the **introductory lesson** students explore the idea of "monster." They draw a "monster" and discuss the characteristics of "monsters." The teacher guides the discussion into a transition explaining that in the book *Monster*, the definition of what a monster is becomes a little less clear, a little less well-defined.

The **reading assignments** are approximately twenty pages each; some are a little shorter while others are a little longer. Students have approximately 15 minutes of pre-reading work to do prior to each reading assignment. This pre-reading work involves reviewing the study questions for the assignment and doing some vocabulary work for several vocabulary words they will encounter in their reading.

The **study guide questions** are fact-based questions; students can find the answers to these questions right in the text. These questions come in two formats: short answer or multiple choice. The best use of these materials is probably to use the short answer version of the questions as study guides for students (since answers will be more complete), and to use the multiple choice version for occasional quizzes. If your school has the appropriate machinery, it might be a good idea to make transparencies of your answer keys for the overhead projector.

The **vocabulary work** is intended to enrich students' vocabularies as well as to aid in the students' understanding of the book. Prior to each reading assignment, students will complete a two-part worksheet for several vocabulary words in the upcoming reading assignment. Part I focuses on students' use of general knowledge and contextual clues by giving the sentence in which the word appears in the text. Students are then to write down what they think the words mean based on the words' usage. Part II nails down the definitions of the words by giving students dictionary definitions of the words and having students match the words to the correct definitions based on the words' contextual usage. Students should then have an understanding of the words when they meet them in the text.

After each reading assignment, students will go back and formulate answers for the study guide questions. Discussion of these questions serves as a **review** of the most important events and ideas presented in the reading assignments.

Students create a film diary of one day in their lives. They have one day in which they explore careers in the criminal justice system and in film-making. They work together in small groups to document and explore the themes of the book. In addition, there is a class period when guest speakers come to talk about the criminal justice system and their roles in it.

Two lessons are devoted to the **extra discussion questions/writing assignments**. These questions focus on interpretation, critical analysis and personal response, employing a variety of thinking skills and adding to the students' understanding of the novel.

After students complete the discussion questions, there is a **vocabulary review** lesson which pulls together all of the fragmented vocabulary lists for the reading assignments and gives students a review of all of the words they have studied.

There are three **writing assignments** in this unit, each with the purpose of informing, persuading, or having students express personal opinions. In the first assignment, students write a film script to document one day in their lives. In assignment number two, students pretend they are Steve, and they write a letter to Petrocelli to convince her that Steve is not a monster. Finally, in the third writing assignment, students respond to the comment Steve wanted to make to his little brother, "Consider all the tomorrows of your life" as it applies to them, personally.

In addition, there is a **nonfiction reading assignment**. Students are required to read a piece of nonfiction related in some way to *Monster*. After reading their nonfiction pieces, students will fill out a worksheet on which they answer questions regarding facts, interpretation, criticism, and personal opinions.

The **review lesson** pulls together all of the aspects of the unit. The teacher is given four or five choices of activities or games to use which all serve the same basic function of reviewing all of the information presented in the unit.

The **unit tests** come in two formats: short answer and multiple choice. As a convenience, two different tests for each format have been included. There is also an advanced short answer unit test which is even more challenging.

There are additional **support materials** included with this unit. The **unit resource materials** section includes suggestions for an in-class library, crossword and word search puzzles related to the novel, and extra vocabulary worksheets. There is a list of **bulletin board ideas** which gives the teacher suggestions for bulletin boards to go along with this unit. In addition, there is a list of **extra class activities** the teacher could choose from to enhance the unit or as a substitution for an exercise the teacher might feel is inappropriate for his/her class. **Answer keys** immediately follow the **reproducible student materials**. The student materials may be reproduced for use in the teacher's classroom without infringement of copyrights. No other portion of this unit may be reproduced without the written consent of Teacher's Pet Publications, Inc.

UNIT OBJECTIVES *Monster*

1. Students will consider the meaning of the word "monster" and discuss its connotations.

2. Students will study point of view throughout the unit.

3. Students will practice reading orally and silently.

4. Students will answer questions to demonstrate their knowledge and understanding of the main events and characters in *Monster*.

5. Students will explore the theme of identity: "Who am I?" as it relates to the book and in their own lives.

6. Students will study careers available in the criminal justice system and in the film industry.

7. Students will look at their own daily lives through the lens of a camera, as they create documentaries of their own daily lives.

8. Students will participate in group activities to gather information, discuss themes, and improve their personal interaction skills.

9. Students will study vocabulary from the book to better understand the book and to improve their own vocabularies.

10. Students will practice their public speaking skills by giving short oral reports.

11. The writing assignments are designed for several purposes:
    a. To check and increase students reading comprehension
    b. To make students think about the ideas presented in the novel
    c. To encourage logical thinking
    d. To provide the opportunity for students to practice good grammar and improve their use of the language
    e. To encourage students' creativity

READING ASSIGNMENTS *Monster*

Date Assigned	Assignment	Completion Date
	Assignment #1 Monday, July 6	
	Assignment #2 Tuesday, July 7 Wednesday, July 8	
	Assignment #3 Thursday, July 9	
	Assignment #4 Friday, July 10 Saturday, July 11 Sunday, July 12	
	Assignment #5 Monday, July 13	
	Assignment #6 Tuesday, July 14 Beginning to "King rests."	
	Assignment #7 Tuesday, July 14 "King rests." to end Friday, July 17 December 5 months later	

UNIT OUTLINE *Monster*

1 Introduction Group Theme Assignment PVR Asst. 1	2 Study ?s 1 Point of View PVR 2	3 Film Documentary Writing Assignment #1	4 Sudy ?s 2 CJ Careers PV 3	5 Complete - Writing Assignment #1 Read 3
6 Study ?s 3 PVR 4 Oral Reading Eval.	7 Speaker	8 Study ?s 4 PVR 5	9 Study ?s 5 Theme Groups PVR 6	10 Study?s 6 PVR 7
11 Study ?s 7 Writing Assignment 2	12 Theme Groups Extra Discussion Questions	13 Extra Discussion Questions Continued Theme Group Discussion	14 Theme Group Discussion Non Fiction Assignment	15 Writing Assignment #3
16 Vocabulary Review	17 Unit Review	18 Unit Test		

P=Preview the Study Questions
V=Do the Vocabulary Worksheet
R=Read

STUDY GUIDE QUESTIONS

STUDY GUIDE QUESTIONS *Monster*

Assignment #1
Beginning - July 6
1. Why is it best to cry at night while someone is screaming?
2. Where is the narrator, at the beginning of the story?
3. What does the narrator feel he has walked into?
4. What does the narrator decide to write in the notebook he is given?
5. What does the narrator name his future film? Why?
6. Who is the narrator?
7. How does Steve envision the opening of his film?
8. Identify :
    Sandra Petrocelli, Kathy O'Brien, James King, Richard "Bobo" Evans, Osvaldo Cruz, Lorelle Henry, Jose Delgado, Steve Harmon
9. Who is on trial for murder?
10. Who is Mr. Sawicki?
11. According to Mr. Sawicki, what is wrong with the film's ending?
12. According to Sandra Petrocelli, who are the monsters in the community?
13. Identify Alguinaldo Nesbitt.
14. According to Kathy O'Brien, what is the wonder and beauty of the American system of justice?
15. Who discovers the body and the missing cigarettes?
16. Why does Sal Zinzi call Detective Gluck with a tip about the robbery?
17. What happens to Tony in the park with Steve?

Assignment #2
Tuesday, July 7 - Wednesday, July 8
1. According to Steve's notes on July 7th, what do they talk about in jail?
2. From whom does Sal Zinzi get information about the robbery?
3. Who tells Wendell Bolden that he was involved in the robbery?
4. What do James King, Peaches, Johnny, and Steve talk about on the stoop?
5. How does Bolden's assault charge get dropped?
6. Why does Jerry want Steve to be Batman?
7. Why do they take away your shoelaces and belt in jail?
8. How does Steve feel in the courtroom?
9. What does the man called Sunset say after reading Steve's play?
10. What does Miss O'Brien say part of her job is?
11. What is Steve's dream?
12. Does Detective Karyl want the death penalty in this case?
13. What is Steve's answer when the older prisoner asks, "Why should you walk?"
14. According to O'Brien, are people innocent until proven guilty?
15. What reason does Osvaldo Cruz give for taking part in the robbery?

Monster Study Questions page 2

Assignment #3
Thursday, July 9
1. What does Acie say about his upcoming verdict?
2. Why does Miss O'Brien put the pictures of Mr. Nesbitt in front of Steve on the table?
3. Why does Steve say he wants to open his shirt when Miss O'Brien looks at him?
4. Why does Steve laugh when King gives him a threatening look?
5. What was Osvaldo's job in the robbery?
6. What three of Osvaldo's actions does O'Brien point out to show he is not a fearful person?
7. What did Mr. Harmon used to dream about for his baby son?
8. What question does Steve ask himself after his father's visit?
9. Steve says he thinks his dad thinks the same as Miss O'Brien does about him. What do they think?
10. What does Detective Williams tell Mrs. Harmon when she asks why they were handcuffing Steve?

Assignment #4
Friday, July 10 - Saturday, July 11 - Sunday, July 12
(July 10)
1. What cheap trick does Petrocelli use on July 10th?
2. What is the guard's reaction to Steve's gagging when cleaning the floors?
3. Describe Steve's reaction to Dr. Moody's testimony about how Mr. Nesbitt actually died. What was James King's reaction to it?

(July 11)
4. How does Steve feel when Miss O'Brien smiles at him?
5. What is Miss O'Brien's response to Steve's telling her he isn't guilty?
6. Does Ernie think he is guilty? Why or why not?
7. What does Mama bring to Steve?
8. What does Steve think as he lies on his cot after Mama's visit?
9. What phrase does King use when talking about the robbery?
10. What is Steve's reaction to King's asking him if he would be the lookout?

(July 12)
11. What happens at the church service in jail?
12. What reason does Steve give for so many fights in jail?
13. Why is it funny to Steve that they don't allow kids in the visiting area?

Monster Study Questions page 3

Assignment #5
Monday, July 13
1. What does Mrs. Henry say in her testimony?
2. Why does Mrs. Henry hesitate to testify against King?
3. Whose gun is used in the shooting?
4. What do Bobo and King do after the robbery?
5. What sign does Steve give Bobo and King that the store is all clear?
6. According to Bobo, was the shooting of Mr. Nesbitt accidental?
7. When Briggs questions Bobo, what point does he try to make?
8. What three points does O'Brien make when questioning Bobo?

Assignment #6
Tuesday, July 14 (part 1 to "King rests.")
1. Why does King's lawyer want to make sure the jury connects him to Steve?
2. Steve says, "Maybe we are here _____."
3. What would Steve have told Jerry if he had been there?
4. What is the essence of Nipping's testimony?
5. Why does O'Brien decide Steve should testify?
6. Why couldn't King testify?
7. What game did O'Brien and Steve play? Why?
8. What does Steve say truth is?
9. What does Inmate 2 say about truth and survival?
10. Does Steve tell the truth on the witness stand?
11. What is Mr. Sawicki's testimony?

Assignment #7
Tuesday, July 14 ("King rests." to the end) - Friday, July 17 - December 5 months later
1. What main points does Briggs make in his closing arguments to the jury?
2. What main points does O'Brien make in her final arguments to the jury?
3. According to Petrocelli, what is this case about?
4. How does Petrocelli describe the crime?
5. What reason does Petrocelli give the jury to urge them to convict Steve Harmon?
(July 17)
6. What does Steve say the reason is that so many guys in jail talk about appeals?
7. What is the jury's verdict for King?
8. What is the jury's verdict for Steve Harmon?
9. What is O'Brien's reaction to Steve's open arms to give her a hug?
10. What is the last image of Steve in the film?
(December, 5 months later)
11. What is Steve doing with his camera? Why?
12. What did Steve's father say to him after the trial?
13. What final question is Steve trying to answer?

STUDY GUIDE QUESTIONS ANSWER KEY *Monster*

<u>Beginning - July 6</u>

1. Why is it best to cry at night while someone is screaming?
   If the others hear you crying, you could be beaten up.

2. Where is the narrator, at the beginning of the story?
   He is in jail.

3. What does the narrator feel he has walked into?
   He feels like he has walked into the middle of a movie with no plot and no beginning.

4. What does the narrator decide to write in the notebook he is given?
   He decides to write down the story of this experience as a film.

5. What does the narrator name his future film? Why?
   He calls it "Monster" because that's what the lady prosecutor called him.

6. Who is the narrator?
   The narrator's name is Steve Harmon.

7. How does Steve envision the opening of his film?
   He sees the title, credits, and a story teaser on the screen, rolling by as in the opening of *Star Wars*.

8. Identify

Sandra Petrocelli	Prosecutor
Kathy O'Brien	Defense Attorney
James King	The Thug
Richard "Bobo" Evans	The Rat
Osvaldo Cruz	Gang Member
Lorelle Henry	Witness
Jose Delgado	Found the body
Steve Harmon	Narrator on trial for murder

9. Who is on trial for murder?
   James King and Steve Harmon are on trial for murder.

10. Who is Mr. Sawicki?
    Mr. Sawicki is the sponsor of the film club Steve belongs to.

11. According to Mr. Sawicki, what is wrong with the film's ending?
    It is predictable.

12. According to Sandra Petrocelli, who are the monsters in the community?
    People who are willing to steal and to kill, people who disregard the rights of others, are monsters.

13. Identify Alguinaldo Nesbitt.
    Mr. Nesbitt is a 55 year-old store owner who is killed in the robbery.

14. According to Kathy O'Brien, what is the wonder and beauty of the American system of justice?
    The wonder and beauty of the system is that it protects citizens but also the accused.

15. Who discovers the body and the missing cigarettes?
    Jose Delgado, a clerk at the store, discovers them.

16. Why does Sal Zinzi call Detective Gluck with a tip about the robbery?
    He wants a break on his jail time in return for the information.

17. What happens to Tony in the park with Steve?
    Steve throws a rock and hits a young woman. The man she is with thinks Tony threw it. He beats up Tony, who didn't run when Steve told him to.

Tuesday, July 7 - Wednesday, July 8
1. According to Steve's notes on July 7th, what do they talk about in jail?
    They talk about hurting people.

2. From whom does Sal Zinzi get information about the robbery?
    He gets his information from Wendell Bolden.

3. Who tells Wendell Bolden that he was involved in the robbery?
    Bobo Evans tells Wendell he was involved.

4. What do James King, Peaches, Johnny, and Steve talk about on the stoop?
    James King was broke and needed to get some money. They talked about how to get the money.

5. How does Bolden's assault charge get dropped?
    He gives the police information about James King and the robbery.

6. Why does Jerry want Steve to be Batman?
    If Steve is Batman, Jerry could be Robin, Batman's helper.

(July 8)
7. Why do they take away your shoelaces and belt in jail?
    They take them away so you can't kill yourself.

8. How does Steve feel in the courtroom?
    He feels like he is not involved with the case–the judge and lawyers and everyone else are doing everything; he does not have an active part.

9. What does the man called Sunset say after reading Steve's play?
    Sunset liked the play, especially the title, "Monster," which he said he would have tattooed on his forehead when he gets out of jail.

10. What does Miss O'Brien say part of her job is?
    She says that part of her job is to make Steve look human in the eyes of the jury.

11. What is Steve's dream?
    He dreams that he tries to ask questions, but no one would hear him. People went about their business like he wasn't there.

12. Does Detective Karyl want the death penalty in this case?
    Yes, he does. He seems to have an active prejudice.

13. What is Steve's answer when the older prisoner asks, "Why should you walk?"
    Steve says, "'Cause I'm a human being. I want a life, too! What's wrong with that?"

14. According to O'Brien, are people innocent until proven guilty?
    She says it depends on how the jury sees the case.

15. What reason does Osvaldo Cruz give for taking part in the robbery?
    He says he is afraid of Bobo, who said he would "cut me and get my moms, too."

Thursday, July 9
1. What does Acie say about his upcoming verdict?
    He says, "All they can do is put me in jail. They can't touch my soul."

2. Why does Miss O'Brien put the pictures of Mr. Nesbitt in front of Steve on the table?
    She wants him to look at them so she can see his reaction.

3. Why does Steve say he wants to open his shirt when Miss O'Brien looks at him?
    "I wanted to open my shirt and tell her to look into my heart to see who I really was, who the real Steve Harmon was."

4. Why does Steve laugh when King gives him a threatening look?
   He says, "They do things to you in jail. You can't scare somebody with a look in here."
   A threatening look is the least of his worries; and he finds King's show of power ridiculous, and laughs at it.

5. What was Osvaldo's job in the robbery?
   His job was to delay anyone chasing Bobo and James after the robbery.

6. What three of Osvaldo's actions does O'Brien point out to show he is not a fearful person?
   She points out that he fought a member of the Diablos gang and cut a stranger in the face to get into the Diablos gang, and he beat up his girlfriend.

7. What did Mr. Harmon used to dream about for his baby son?
   He thought about baby Steve growing up, going to college, and playing football.

8. What question does Steve ask himself after his father's visit?
   He asks himself, "What did I do? What did I do?"

9. Steve says he thinks his dad thinks the same as Miss O'Brien does about him. What do they think?
   Steve thinks his dad and Miss O'Brien both think that the jury will not see a difference between him and the bad guys taking the stand.

10. What does Detective Williams tell Mrs. Harmon when she asks why they were handcuffing Steve?
    He says, "Ma'am, it's just routine. Don't worry about it."

Friday, July 10 - Saturday, July 11 - Sunday, July 12
(July 10)
1. What cheap trick does Petrocelli use on July 10th?
   She brings up the photos again so the jury will think about them over the weekend.

2. What is the guard's reaction to Steve's gagging when cleaning the floors?
   He said, "You vomit–you just got more to clean up!"

3. Describe Steve's reaction to Dr. Moody's testimony about how Mr. Nesbitt actually died. What was James King's reaction to it?
   Steve catches his breath sharply. King listens to it without any sign of caring.

(July 11)
4. How does Steve feel when Miss O'Brien smiles at him?
   He says he is embarrassed that a smile should mean so much.

5. What is Miss O'Brien's response to Steve's telling her he isn't guilty?
   She said he should have said, "I didn't do it."

6. Does Ernie think he is guilty? Why or why not?
   Ernie doesn't think he is guilty because he didn't actually take anything out of the store.

7. What does Mama bring to Steve?
   She brings him a Bible with a passage marked she thought would help him.

8. What does Steve think as he lies on his cot after Mama's visit?
   He thinks, "I could still feel Mama's pain. And I knew she felt that I didn't do anything wrong. It was me who wasn't sure. It was me who lay on the cot wondering if I was fooling myself."

9. What phrase does King use when talking about the robbery?
   He calls it "getting paid."

10. What is Steve's reaction to King's asking him if he would be the lookout?
    He looks away.

(July 12)
11. What happens at the church service in jail?
    Two guys start fighting. The guards break it up and lock everyone back in their cells.

12. What reason does Steve give for so many fights in jail?
    He says, "In here all you have going for you is the little surface stuff. . . . you have to protect that."

13. Why is it funny to Steve that they don't allow kids in the visiting area?
    He thinks it's funny that if he weren't locked up, he wouldn't even be allowed in the visitor's area.

Monday, July 13
1. What does Mrs. Henry say in her testimony?
   She says she saw King arguing with the store owner on December 22nd, and she then left the store because she thought there might be trouble.

2. Why does Mrs. Henry hesitate to testify against King?
   She "has trouble" testifying against a Black man.

3. Whose gun is used in the shooting?
   Mr. Nesbitt's gun is used. The robbers were not armed.

4. What do Bobo and King do after the robbery?
   They go to a fast food restaurant to get fried chicken, wedgies, and sodas.

5. What sign does Steve give Bobo and King that the store is all clear?
   He gives no sign. He just walked out, and they figured it was all right.

6. According to Bobo, was the shooting of Mr. Nesbitt accidental?
   No, it wasn't. King said he "had to light him up because he was trying to muscle him."

7. When Briggs questions Bobo, what point does he try to make?
   Briggs tries to make the point that Bobo actually killed Mr. Nesbitt and is trying to blame it on King.

8. What three points does O'Brien make when questioning Bobo?
   - Steve had no prior or subsequent connection with Bobo.
   - King and Bobo were "laying low" alone.
   - Steve received no money.

Tuesday, July 14 (part 1 to "King rests.")
1. Why does King's lawyer want to make sure the jury connects him to Steve?
   Steve looks like a pretty decent guy.

2. Steve says, "Maybe we are here _____."
   Maybe we are here because we lie to ourselves."

3. What would Steve have told Jerry if he had been there?
   "Think about all the tomorrows of your life."

4. What is the essence of Nipping's testimony?
   King is left-handed.

5. Why does O'Brien decide Steve should testify?
   She wants to put as much distance between Steve and King as possible, and to present Steve as someone the jurors can believe in.

6. Why couldn't King testify?
   The prosecution "can use his own statements against him, and he's cooked."

7. What game did O'Brien and Steve play? Why?
   They played cup up/cup down to help train Steve how to answer questions.

8. What does Steve say truth is?
    He says, "Truth is truth. It's what you know to be right."

9. What does Inmate 2 say about truth and survival?
    He says, "Truth is something you gave up when you were out there in the street. Now you are talking survival."

10. Does Steve tell the truth on the witness stand?
    No, he doesn't.

11. What is Mr. Sawicki's testimony?
    He testifies that Steve is an outstanding young man: talented, bright, compassionate, and honest.

<u>Tuesday, July 14 ("King rests." to the end) - Friday, July 17 - December 5 months later</u>
1. What main points does Briggs make in his closing arguments to the jury?
    - Bobo implicates King because the police have him on a criminal matter and have offered him a deal if he comes here and implicates someone else.
    - Bobo's character is that of a criminal, a drug dealer, and a robber.
    - The prosecution did not produce any witnesses to the murder.
    - Mrs. Henry's mind was on her granddaughter; she could have been mistaken about King's identity.
    - Mrs. Moore said King was at her house at the time of the robbery. We can't assume everyone related to the accused would lie.
    - This case is about whether or not you believe people who are admitted participants in this crime and who are saving their own hides. If you believe that their positions, their stated characters, so taint their testimony that everything they say is well within the area of reasonable doubt, then you have no choice but to find Mr. King not guilty.

2. What main points does O'Brien make in her final arguments to the jury?
    - The State did not establish any conversation about the robbery between Mr. Harmon and anyone else involved.
    - The State did not even suggest that Mr. Harmon was in the store at the time of the robbery.
    - Mr. Harmon was not with Bobo and King eating chicken after the crime.
    - Mr. Harmon did not receive any of the loot.
    - Mr. Evans and Mr. Cruz implicate Mr. Harmon out of self-interest, to get reduced sentences.
    - To Mr. Evans, Mr. Nesbitt was just a "get over," and that's what Steve is to him, too.
    - Mr. Harmon answered questions openly and honestly on the stand and is of a much better character than the others who took the stand.
    - Mrs. Henry did not identify Steve as being in the store.

3. According to Petrocelli, what is this case about?
   "This case is about a crime that was committed on the 22nd of December, in which an innocent man, Alguinaldo Nesbitt, was brutally murdered."

4. How does Petrocelli describe the crime?
   "This was a botched robbery in which the perpetrators actually took very little money and a few cartons of cigarettes. And, oh, yes, the life of a good man, Alguinaldo Nesbitt."

5. What reason does Petrocelli give the jury to urge them to convict Steve Harmon?
   "Steve Harmon was part of the plan that caused the death of Alguinaldo Nesbitt. . . . He made a moral decision to participate in this "getover." He wanted to "get paid" with everybody else. He is as guilty as everybody else, no matter how many moral hairs he can split. His participation made the crime easier. His willingness to check out the store, no matter how poorly he did it, was one of those causative factors that resulted in the death of Mr. Nesbitt.

(July 17)
6. What does Steve say the reason is that so many guys in jail talk about appeals?
   "They want to continue the argument, and the system says it's over."

7. What is the jury's verdict for King?
   Guilty

8. What is the jury's verdict for Steve Harmon?
   Not guilty.

9. What is O'Brien's reaction to Steve's open arms to give her a hug?
   She stiffens and turns to pick up papers on the table.

10. What is the last image of Steve in the film?
    He turns towards the camera with outstretched arms. The picture turns black and white and grainy/distorted. He looks like a monster.

(December, 5 months later)
11. What is Steve doing with his camera? Why?
    He is making films of himself from all different angles & in different clothes. He wants to know who he is. "I want to look at myself a thousand times to look for one true image."

12. What did Steve's father say to him after the trial?
    He was glad Steve didn't have to go to jail.

13. What final question is Steve trying to answer?
    What did Miss O'Brien see that caused her to turn away from him at the end of the trial?

MULTIPLE CHOICE STUDY/QUIZ QUESTIONS
Monster

Assignment #1

Beginning - July 6

1. Why is it best to cry at night while someone is screaming?
    A. If the guards hear you, they will pick on you the next day.
    B. If the others hear you crying, you could be beaten up.
    C. If you start crying during the day when you should be working, it counts against you.
    D. A & B

2. Where is the narrator, at the beginning of the story?
    A. He is in film class.
    B. He is in the park.
    C. He is on the street.
    D. He is in jail.

3. What does the narrator feel he has walked into?
    A. He feels like he has walked into a wall.
    B. He feels like he has walked into a fog.
    C. He feels like he has walked into the middle of a movie with no plot and no beginning.
    D. He feels like he has walked into a circus.

4. What does the narrator decide to write in the notebook he is given?
    A. He decides to write down his regrets.
    B. He decides to write down a mark for each day he is in jail.
    C. He decides to write down the story of this experience as a film.
    D. He decides to write down letters to his family.

5. What does the narrator name his future film? Why?
    A. He calls it "Monster" because that's what the lady prosecutor called him.
    B. He calls it "Monster" because he feels like a monster.
    C. He calls it "Monster" because he feels surrounded by monsters in jail.
    D. He calls it "Monster" because the events are so distorted as he thinks about them.

6. Who is the narrator?
    A. The narrator is no one involved with the story. It's in 3rd person.
    B. The narrator is Steve Harmon.
    C. The narrator is James King.
    D. The narrator is Jose Delgado.

Monster Multiple Choice Questions for Assignment 1 page 2

7. How does Steve envision the opening of his film?
    A. He sees the title, credits, and a story teaser on the screen, rolling by as in the opening of *Star Wars*.
    B. He sees his film starting with a photograph of Mr. Nisbett's murdered body.
    C. He sees the credits being pushed on and off the screen by a monster.
    D. He sees the film opening with the camera panning over the jury in close-ups.

8. Identify
    ___ Sandra Petrocelli   A. Witness
    ___ Kathy O'Brien   B. Found the body
    ___ James King   C. Gang Member
    ___ Richard "Bobo" Evans   D. Narrator on trial for murder
    ___ Osvaldo Cruz   E. Defense Attorney
    ___ Lorelle Henry   F. The Rat
    ___ Jose Delgado   G. The Thug
    ___ Steve Harmon   H. Prosecutor

9. Who is on trial for murder?
    A. Osvaldo Cruz and James King
    B. Bobo Evans and Steve Harmon
    C. Bobo Evans and James King
    D. James King and Steve Harmon

10. Who is Mr. Sawicki?
    A. He is a detective.
    B. He owned a store and was murdered during a robbery.
    C. He is the sponsor of the film club Steve belongs to.
    D. He is Steve's father.

11. According to Mr. Sawicki, what is wrong with the film's ending?
    A. It doesn't resolve the conflicts.
    B. It is too abrupt.
    C. It leaves the audience feeling too sad.
    D. It is predictable.

12. According to Sandra Petrocelli, who are the monsters in the community?
    A. Defense attorneys who try to keep murderers out of jail
    B. People who are willing to steal and to kill; people who disregard the rights of others
    C. People who are prejudiced
    D. People who don't bother to see others for who they really are

Monster Multiple Choice Questions for Assignment 1 page 3

13. Identify Alguinaldo Nesbitt.
    A. Mr. Nesbitt is a witness to the murder.
    B. Mr. Nesbitt is a 55 year-old store owner who is killed in the robbery.
    C. Mr. Nesbitt is King's attorney.
    D. Mr. Nesbitt is the detective Osvaldo Cruz gives information to.

14. According to Kathy O'Brien, what is the wonder and beauty of the American system of justice?
    A. It always manages to punish the guilty and set innocent people free.
    B. It usually surpasses her lofty expectations.
    C. It protects citizens but also the accused.
    D. It dispenses equal justice for all.

15. Who discovers the body and the missing cigarettes?
    A. Jose Delgado, a clerk at the store, discovers them.
    B. Mrs. Henry, a shopper, discovers them.
    C. Detective Gluck discovers them.
    D. Mrs. Nesbitt, the wife of the store owner, discovers them.

16. Why does Sal Zinzi call Detective Gluck with a tip about the robbery?
    A. He owes Gluck a favor for previously getting his jail time reduced.
    B. He wants to get even with James King by ratting him out to the police.
    C. He wants a break on his jail time in return for the information.
    D. He is hoping for a part of the reward money.

17. What happens to Tony in the park with Steve?
    A. Tony throws a stone and hits a woman passing by.
    B. Tony is beaten up for something Steve did.
    C. Tony and Steve are beaten up by some members of the Diablo gang.
    D. A & B

Monster Multiple Choice Questions for Assignment 2

Assignment #2
Tuesday, July 7 - Wednesday, July 8
1. According to Steve's notes on July 7th, what do they talk about in jail?
    A. They talk about missing their families.
    B. They talk about when they were kids.
    C. They talk about hurting people.
    D. They talk about escaping.

2. From whom does Sal Zinzi get information about the robbery?
    A. He gets his information from Wendell Bolden.
    B. He gets his information from Osvaldo Cruz.
    C. He gets his information from Steven.
    D. He gets his information from Bobo Evans.

3. Who tells Wendell Bolden that he was involved in the robbery?
    A. Steven
    B. James
    C. Osvaldo
    D. Bobo

4. What do James King, Peaches, Johnny, and Steve talk about on the stoop?
    A. They talk about how to get some money.
    B. They plan the robbery.
    C. They talk about how they used to play together when they were kids, and how things seem so much more complicated now than then.
    D. They talk about respect.

5. How does Bolden's assault charge get dropped?
    A. His lawyer finds a technicality in the charging documents that would allow him to get off.
    B. He gives the police information about James King and the robbery.
    C. He gives Karyl information about the Diablos gang.
    D. His testimony connects Steven and James King.

6. Why does Jerry want Steve to be Batman?
    A. He wants his brother to be a superhero instead of a criminal.
    B. If Steve is Batman, Jerry could be Robin, Batman's helper.
    C. Everyone knows who Batman is.
    D. Jerry is scared of the dark at night. Batman is the perfect protector for him.

Monster Multiple Choice Questions Assignment 2 page 2

(July 8)
7. According to Steve, why do they take away your shoelaces and belt in jail?
    A. It is a part of taking away your personal identity, to make you like everyone else.
    B. Shoelaces and belts are potential weapons the inmates could use in fights or to hurt the guards.
    C. They donate them to charity since you don't need them anymore.
    D. They take them away so you can't kill yourself.

8. How does Steve feel in the courtroom?
    A. He feels uncomfortable because everyone keeps looking at him like he's guilty.
    B. He feels like he can't breathe; like all the walls are closing in on him.
    C. He feels like he is not involved with the case–the judge and lawyers and everyone else are doing everything; he does not have an active part.
    D. He feels like the prosecutor and O'Brien have already cut a deal between themselves and they are just going through the motions of a trial, already knowing the outcome will be a guilty verdict.

9. What does the man called Sunset say after reading Steve's play?
    A. Sunset liked the play, especially the title, "Monster," which he said he would have tattooed on his forehead when he gets out of jail.
    B. He hates it because "it doesn't have nothin' to do with anythin' that is real."
    C. Sunset says, "Man, I don' know what you doin' here. You coulda made somethin' of youself. You coulda been somebody."
    D. "You're just foolin' yourself, man. Ain't nobody cares about this stuff. We just rot in jail and ain't nobody cares."

10. What does Miss O'Brien say part of her job is?
    A. Part of her job is to exploit any little cracks in the prosecutor's case.
    B. Part of her job is to figure out whether or not Steve is really guilty.
    C. Part of her job is to create monsters.
    D. Part of her job is to make Steve look human in the eyes of the jury.

11. What is Steve's dream?
    A. He dreams he becomes a big film-maker star. In an interview a reporter asks him about the time he spent in jail.
    B. He dreams that he tries to ask questions, but no one would hear him. People went about their business like he wasn't there.
    C. He dreams that Osvaldo and Bobo meet him in the park and beat him to death.
    D. He dreams Mr. Nesbitt points at him, yelling, "YOU! YOU! You killed me!"

Monster Multiple Choice Questions Assignment 2 page 3

12. Does Detective Karyl want the death penalty in this case?
    A. Yes, he does. He seems to have an active prejudice.
    B. No, he doesn't. He doesn't believe in the death penalty for any case.
    C. He wants to see James King get the death penalty, but he doesn't think Steven should.
    D. We aren't given enough information to tell what he really thinks.

13. What is Steve's answer when the older prisoner asks, "Why should you walk?"
    A. Steve says, "'Cause I didn't do it!"
    B. Steve says, "I'm not like the others! I never been in trouble before."
    C. Steve says, "Why shouldn't I? I'm as good as the next guy. Everybody messes up sometime, sooner or later."
    D. Steve says, "'Cause I'm a human being. I want a life, too! What's wrong with that?"

14. According to O'Brien, are people innocent until proven guilty?
    A. She says people ARE innocent until proven guilty; that's the hallmark of our judicial system.
    B. She says she never met a defendant who didn't do what they were accused of doing. The guilty get prosecuted; the innocent never get arrested.
    C. She says it depends on how the jury sees the case.
    D. She says that's just a dusty old phrase that no one ever pays attention to anymore.

15. What reason does Osvaldo Cruz give for taking part in the robbery?
    A. He says he needed the cash. He was flat broke.
    B. He says he couldn't help himself; he was high and went along for the ride.
    C. He says he was afraid of Bobo, who said he would "cut me and get my moms, too."
    D. He says "that old man had it coming."

Monster Multiple Choice Questions Assignment 3

Assignment #3
Thursday, July 9
1. What does Acie say about his upcoming verdict?
    A. He says, "All they can do is put me in jail. They can't touch my soul."
    B. He says, "It is what it is."
    C. He says, "I'm sacred, man. I never meant to be here. I don't know what to do."
    D. He says, "Ain't nobody in the whole system lookin' out for us. All they see is another piece of trouble. Ain't none of us real to them. They don't care."

2. Why does Miss O'Brien put the pictures of Mr. Nesbitt in front of Steve on the table?
    A. She wants him to realize what he has done, to confess, and to be sorry.
    B. She wants him to look at them so she can see his reaction.
    C. She thinks they might be helpful to him in his film.
    D. She knows the photos will upset him. She wants the jury to see him agitated and uneasy.

3. Why does Steve say he wants to open his shirt when Miss O'Brien looks at him?
    A. "I wanted to open my shirt and tell her to look into my heart to see who I really was, who the real Steve Harmon was."
    B. "I wanted to open my shirt and tell her to just go ahead and rip out my heart now, because that's what this is like–and at least it would be over."
    C. "I wanted to open my shirt, rip it off, and throw it at her. Maybe then she'd wake up from this fog that keeps her from seeing the truth!"
    D. "I wanted to open up my shirt, show her I'm flesh and blood, show her I'm not just a case number, not just another bad act on the courtroom stage."

4. Why does Steve laugh when King gives him a threatening look?
    A. He says, "They do things to you in jail. You can't scare somebody with a look in here." A threatening look is the least of his worries; and he finds King's show of power ridiculous, and laughs at it.
    B. Steve is mentally picturing King how he would portray him as a clown in his movie.
    C. Being in jail has made Steve more bold. He doesn't feel like he has to take threats seriously anymore because he no longer cares what happens to himself anymore.
    D. King reminds Steve of the Penguin in an old Batman movie. He pictures himself as Batman and visualizes the words "POW!" "BAM!" "POOF!" on the screen all around King.

5. What was Osvaldo's job in the robbery?
    A. His job was to make sure the store was empty.
    B. His job was to grab the money.
    C. His job was to be a witness but to tell the police all the wrong information.
    D. His job was to delay anyone chasing Bobo and James after the robbery.

Monster Multiple Choice Questions Assignment 3 page 2

6. Which of these is NOT one of Osvaldo's actions that O'Brien points out to show he is not a fearful person?
    A. He fought a member of the Diablos gang.
    B. He cut a stranger in the face.
    C. He beat up Tony in the park.
    D. He beat up his girlfriend.

7. What did Mr. Harmon used to dream about for his baby son?
    A. He thought about baby Steve becoming a lawyer, a champion of justice.
    B. He thought about baby Steve growing up, going to college, and playing football.
    C. He thought about baby Steve coming back to clean up the neighborhood, as a cop.
    D. He thought about baby Steve moving to New York City to become a film director.

8. What question does Steve ask himself after his father's visit?
    A. "How can I ever become the man he wants me to be?"
    B. "What did I do? What did I do?"
    C. "What'll they serve for dinner tonight?"
    D. "Who am I?"

9. Steve says he thinks his dad thinks the same as Miss O'Brien does about him. What do they think?
    A. They think he's lost–gone down a bad road that he won't recover from.
    B. They think he IS a monster who killed someone for a little money and some cigarettes.
    C. They think there is hope for him if he can get a break on this one case.
    D. They think that the jury will not see a difference between him and the bad guys taking the stand.

10. What does Detective Williams tell Mrs. Harmon when she asks why they were handcuffing Steve?
    A. He says, "Ma'am, it's just routine. Don't worry about it."
    B. He says, "He killed a guy in a robbery on December 22nd."
    C. He tells her she should get her coat and come along with them.
    D. He tells Mrs. Harmon she should go get a good lawyer.

Monster Multiple Choice Questions Assignment 4

Assignment #4
<u>Friday, July 10 - Saturday, July 11 - Sunday, July 12</u>
(July 10)
1. What cheap trick does Petrocelli use on July 10th?
    A. She tells Steve his parents were in a car accident.
    B. She wears a low-cut blouse.
    C. She asks the judge for a continuance.
    D. She brings up the photos again so the jury will think about them over the weekend.

2. What is the guard's reaction to Steve's gagging when cleaning the floors?
    A. He laughed at Steve.
    B. He started gagging, too, and vomited on the floor.
    C. He said, "You vomit–you just got more to clean up!"
    D. He said, "What a pansy! Not even man enough to clean a floor without gagging!"

3. Describe Steve's reaction to Dr. Moody's testimony about how Mr. Nesbitt actually died. What was James King's reaction to it?
    A. Steve starts to cry. King catches his breath sharply.
    B. Steve catches his breath sharply. King listens to it without any sign of caring.
    C. Steve cringes. King laughs.
    D. Steve looks solemn. King smirks.

(July 11)
4. How does Steve feel when Miss O'Brien smiles at him?
    A. It makes him feel sick to his stomach. He isn't sure why.
    B. He feels uneasy; he isn't sure if she is making fun of him or genuinely likes him.
    C. He says he is embarrassed that a smile should mean so much.
    D. It makes him want to believe that she believes in him.

5. What is Miss O'Brien's response to Steve's telling her he isn't guilty?
    A. She says he should have said, "I didn't do it."
    B. She turns away in silence.
    C. She tells him she doesn't believe him, that he is, in fact, a monster.
    D. She heaves a sigh of relief because it confirms what she has thought all along.

6. Does Ernie think he is guilty? Why or why not?
    A. Ernie thinks he is guilty because he knows he did it.
    B. Ernie doesn't think he is guilty because he didn't actually take anything out of the store.
    C. Ernie doesn't think he's guilty because he's a good guy at heart.
    D. Ernie thinks he's guilty because he intended to do it.

Monster Multiple Choice Questions Assignment 4 page 2

7. What does Mama bring to Steve?
    A. She brings him magazines about film making.
    B. She brings him his mail from home.
    C. She brings him a cake.
    D. She brings him a Bible with a passage marked she thought would help him.

8. What does Steve think as he lies on his cot after Mama's visit?
    A. He thinks about how good Mama has been to him and how he has let her down. He wishes he hadn't gotten into this mess and that he could make her proud again.
    B. He thinks his being in this situation is Mama's fault. She doesn't even know who he is or what he does. If she had cared more and paid more attention to him, he wouldn't be in this mess.
    C. He thinks, "I know Mama cares. I just wish she's leave me alone here. Alone with my thoughts, alone with my pain. I don't think I could stand another visit from Mama."
    D. He thinks, "I could still feel Mama's pain. And I knew she felt that I didn't do anything wrong. It was me who wasn't sure. It was me who lay on the cot wondering if I was fooling myself."

9. What phrase does King use when talking about the robbery?
    A. He calls it "doing it."
    B. He calls it "changing coin."
    C. He calls it "getting paid."
    D. He calls it "dropping down."

10. What is Steve's reaction to King's asking him if he would be the lookout?
    A. He looks away.
    B. He laughs.
    C. He gathers all of his strength and hits King in the face.
    D. He thanks King for the opportunity to prove himself.

(July 12)
11. What happens at the church service in jail?
    A. One of the inmates attacks the preacher.
    B. Two guys start fighting. The guards break it up and lock everyone back in their cells.
    C. One inmate sets another on fire with a candle.
    D. The preacher singles out Steve, calling for him to repent.

Monster Multiple Choice Questions Assignment 4 page 3

12. What reason does Steve give for so many fights in jail?
    A. He says, "Everyone is so close together, so in each other's faces. It makes everyone edgy. It just has to come out somewhere."
    B. He says, "In here all you have going for you is the little surface stuff. . . . you have to protect that."
    C. He says, "Guys in here have lost everything. Family. Friends. Hope. When there's nothing left in life, there's nothing left but the physical, the fight, the survival."
    D. He says, "Anger builds up. You're angry at being forced into doing something you didn't want to do. And angry that you got caught. And angry that people who aren't like you, in here, don't even look at you anymore. And you're angry at yourself."

13. Why is it funny to Steve that they don't allow kids in the visiting area?
    A. He thinks kids should be allowed to come in and see what it is to be in jail so they won't do stuff that will put them there.
    B. He can visualize a film cartoon with kids shooting nerf guns and being rowdy all over the jail's visiting area.
    C. He thinks it's funny because he knows the kids are probably safer in the visitor's area than at home in their neighborhood.
    D. He thinks it's funny that if he weren't locked up, he wouldn't even be allowed in the visitor's area.

Monster Multiple Choice Questions Assignment 5

Assignment #5
<u>Monday, July 13</u>
1. Which of these statements does Mrs. Henry NOT say in her testimony?
    A. She says she saw King arguing with the store owner on December 22nd.
    B. She left the store because she thought there might be trouble.
    C. She was at the store to buy medicine for her granddaughter.
    D. She saw Steve in the store.

2. Why does Mrs. Henry hesitate to testify against King?
    A. She "has trouble" testifying against a Black man.
    B. She is afraid of him.
    C. She is his aunt.
    D. She isn't sure she identified the right person.

3. Whose gun is used in the shooting?
    A. Steve Harmon's
    B. Mr. Nesbitt's
    C. James King's
    D. Bobo Evans's

4. What do Bobo and King do after the robbery?
    A. They go to a fast food restaurant to get fried chicken, wedgies, and sodas.
    B. They "lay low" in the park.
    C. They go home.
    D. They return to the crime scene and pretend like they weren't involved.

5. What sign does Steve give Bobo and King that the store is all clear?
    A. He nods as he exits the store.
    B. He gives a "thumbs up."
    C. He straightens his hat.
    D. He gives no sign. He just walks out, and they figure it was all right.

6. According to Bobo, was the shooting of Mr. Nesbitt accidental?
    A. Yes, he said the gun "just went off" when King and Nesbitt were wrestling.
    B. Yes, Nesbitt fired his gun as King was bumping into him; Nesbitt actually shot himself.
    C. No, it wasn't. King said he "had to light him up because he was trying to muscle him."
    D. No, it wasn't. Bobo testified that Nesbitt drew first, and King shot him in self-defense.

Monster Multiple Choice Questions Assignment 5 page 2

7. When Briggs questions Bobo, what point does he try to make?
    A. Bobo forced King to do the robbery and kill Mr. Nesbitt.
    B. Bobo knew Mr. Nesbitt had the gun and would use it.
    C. Bobo actually killed Mr. Nesbitt and is trying to blame it on King.
    D. Bobo is a lying weasel.

8. Which of these points does O'Brien NOT make when questioning Bobo?
    A. Steve had no prior or subsequent connection with Bobo.
    B. Steve was not in the store at the time of the incident.
    C. King and Bobo were "laying low" alone.
    D. Steve received no money.

Monster Multiple Choice Questions Assignment 6

Assignment #6
Tuesday, July 14 (part 1 to "King rests.")
1. Why does King's lawyer want to make sure the jury connects him to Steve?
    A. He wants to make sure King doesn't take the fall for the murder alone.
    B. Steve looks like a pretty decent guy.
    C. Steve can prove King didn't do it.
    D. The jury seems to like Steve.

2. Steve says, "Maybe we are here _____."
    A. to show our humanity
    B. as actors in the film of life
    C. simply because someone has to be
    D. because we lie to ourselves

3. What would Steve have told Jerry if he had been there?
    A. "I'm not guilty."
    B. "Be a better son to Mama than I have been."
    C. "Think about all the tomorrows of your life."
    D. "I'm sorry."

4. What is the essence of Nipping's testimony?
    A. King is left-handed.
    B. King is a criminal and a liar.
    C. King had a gun.
    D. King had bragged about killing the store owner.

5. Why does O'Brien decide Steve should testify?
    A. The others testifying are making him look bad.
    B. She wants to hear the truth, under oath, directly from Steve.
    C. O'Brien wants the jury to see Steve is sorry for participating in the robbery/murder.
    D. She wants to put as much distance between Steve and King as possible, and to present Steve as someone the jurors can believe in.

6. Why couldn't King testify?
    A. No one would believe him.
    B. The prosecution can use his own statements against him, and that would practically assure a guilty verdict.
    C. The jury would be afraid of him.
    D. It was a part of his plea bargain and reduced sentence, that he would not testify.

Monster Multiple Choice Questions Assignment 6 Page 2

7. What game did O'Brien and Steve play? Why?
    A. They played cat and mouse. She would ask a question, and he would avoid answering.
    B. O'Brien taught him how to play poker so he would fit in with the inmates.
    C. They played cup up/cup down to help train Steve how to answer questions.
    D. They played the ink-blot game. O'Brien wanted to get some insight into Steve's thinking.

8. What does Steve say truth is?
    A. He says, "Truth is what people make it."
    B. He says, "Truth is truth. It's what you know to be right."
    C. He says, "Truth is just a matter of perception. The truth of a thing is different to different people involved."
    D. He says, "Truth is unattainable. No one can know what is true."

9. What does Inmate 2 say about truth and survival?
    A. He says, "If you know the truth, you have a chance for survival."
    B. He says, "Truth is something you gave up when you were out there in the street. Now you are talking survival."
    C. He says, "Pray that you don't know the truth. It will destroy you; you will not survive."
    D. He says, "Survival is the only truth in here."

10. Does Steve tell the truth on the witness stand?
    A. No
    B. Yes
    C. It depends on the jury.
    D. He thought he did.

11. What is NOT a part of Mr. Sawicki's testimony?
    A. Steve is an outstanding young man.
    B. Steve is talented, bright, & compassionate.
    C. Steve is honest.
    D. Steve is a great big brother.

Monster Multiple Choice Questions Assignment 7

Assignment #7
Tuesday, July 14 ("King rests." to the end) - Friday, July 17 - December 5 months later

1. What main point is NOT a part of Briggs's closing arguments to the jury?
    A. Bobo implicates King because the police have him on a criminal matter and have offered him a deal if he comes here and implicates someone else.
    B. Mrs. Henry's mind was on her granddaughter; she could have been mistaken about King's identity.
    C. King was desperate to acquire some money; he was broke.
    D. This case is about whether or not you believe people who are admitted participants in this crime and who are saving their own hides. If you believe that their positions, their stated characters, so taint their testimony that everything they say is well within the area of reasonable doubt, then you have no choice but to find Mr. King not guilty.

2. What main point is NOT one O'Brien makes in her final arguments to the jury?
    A. The State did not even suggest that Mr. Harmon was in the store at the time of the robbery.
    B. Mr. Harmon was not with Bobo and King eating chicken after the crime.
    C. Steve has no prior criminal record.
    D. Mr. Harmon answered questions openly and honestly on the stand and is of a much better character than the others who took the stand.

3. According to Petrocelli, what is this case about?
    A. "This case is about a crime that was committed on the 22nd of December, in which an innocent man, Alguinaldo Nesbitt, was brutally murdered."
    B. "This case is about monsters."
    C. "In this case, we're not just trying criminals. Our whole justice system is on trial here. Deals for information, criminals racing to see who can rat out the other first to get a reduced sentence. What has our court system come to? With your verdict you're not only judging the facts of the case; you are judging our entire justice system."
    D. "This case is about truth and survival. Who is telling the truth, and who is just trying to survive?"

4. How does Petrocelli describe the crime?
    A. "This was a carefully planned, professionally executed robbery and murder."
    B. "This was a botched robbery in which the perpetrators actually took very little money and a few cartons of cigarettes. And, oh, yes, the life of a good man, Alguinaldo Nesbitt."
    C. "This monstrous crime was a thoughtless act, a selfish act, an act totally without reason, excuse, or principle."
    D. "These monsters traded the life of Alguinaldo Nesbitt for some money and cigarettes. What could be worse? This crime is the epitome of selfishness and cruelty and cannot go unpunished."

Monster Multiple Choice Questions Assignment 7 Page 2

5. Which of these is NOT a reason Petrocelli gives the jury to urge them to convict Steve Harmon?
    A. He made a moral decision to participate in this "getover."
    B. He wanted to "get paid" with everybody else.
    C. His willingness to check out the store, no matter how poorly he did it, was one of the factors that resulted in the death of Mr. Nesbitt.
    D. Mrs. Henry placed him at the scene of the crime.

(July 17)
6. What does Steve say the reason is that so many guys in jail talk about appeals?
    A. "It's the only safe subject, that you won't get beat up for."
    B. "They want to continue the argument, and the system says it's over."
    C. "Appeals are the only hope for freedom."
    D. "Searching for a way to appeal is like searching for truth."

7. What is the jury's verdict for King?
    A. Guilty
    B. Not guilty

8. What is the jury's verdict for Steve Harmon?
    A. Guilty
    B. Not guilty

9. What is O'Brien's reaction to Steve's open arms to give her a hug?
    A. At first she reaches to hug him back, but then turns away.
    B. She gives him a brief and professional hug then turns away.
    C. She stiffens and turns to pick up papers on the table.
    D. O'Brien says, "Goodbye. Good luck." And she walks past him.

10. What is the last image of Steve in the film?
    A. He is alone on the courthouse steps.
    B. He is holding his camera, filming an image of himself in a mirror.
    C. He is home with his family, playing Batman and Robin with Jerry.
    D. He turns towards the camera with outstretched arms. The picture turns grainy/distorted. He looks like a monster.

Monster Multiple Choice Questions Assignment 7 Page 3

(December, 5 months later)

11. What is Steve doing with his camera? Why?
    - A. He is making films of himself from all different angles & in different clothes. He says, "I want to look at myself a thousand times to look for one true image."
    - B. He is making a film of his experiences for film class.
    - C. He is filming his family. He has recognized how precious they are to him and he wants their daily life to be on film so he can look at it and remember the truth of his life forever.
    - D. He is taking pictures of himself to send his true images to Miss O'Brien.

12. What did Steve's father say to him after the trial?
    - A. "I knew you would be all right."
    - B. He said to remember all the tomorrows you have ahead.
    - C. He said he was glad Steve didn't have to go to jail.
    - D. He said, "Justice isn't always served best by truth."

13. What final question is Steve trying to answer?
    - A. Why did I agree to go check out the store?
    - B. What did Miss O'Brien see that caused her to turn away from me?
    - C. What will I do with my life now?
    - D. What is truth?

ANSWER KEY: STUDY QUESTIONS *Monster*

	1	2	3	4	5	6	7
1	B	C	A	D	D	B	C
2	D	A	B	C	A	D	C
3	C	D	A	B	B	C	A
4	C	A	A	C	A	A	B
5	A	B	D	A	D	D	D
6	B	B	C	B	C	B	B
7	A	D	B	D	C	C	A
8	H E G F C A B D	C	B	D	B	B	B
9	D	A	D	C		B	C
10	C	D	A	A		A	D
11	D	B		B		D	A
12	B	A		B			C
13	B	D		D			B
14	C	C					
15	A	C					
16	C						
17	B						

VOCABULARY WORKSHEETS

VOCABULARY ASSIGNMENT 1 *Monster*

Part I: Using Prior Knowledge and Contextual Clues

Below are the sentences in which the vocabulary words appear in the text. Read the sentence. Use any clues you can find in the sentence combined with your prior knowledge, and write what you think the underlined words mean on the lines provided.

1. Early morning in CELL BLOCK D, MANHATTAN DETENTION CENTER. Camera goes slowly down grim, gray <u>corridor</u>.

2. There are sounds of inmates yelling from cell to cell; much of it is <u>obscene</u>.

3. CUT TO: STEVE, who is seated on a low bench. He is handcuffed to a U-bolt put in the bench for that purpose. . . . They <u>unshackle</u> STEVE and take him toward door.

4. ASA BRIGGS, the lead <u>counsel</u> for the defense of JAMES KING, stands.

5. I'm ruling the kid's testimony is <u>admissible</u>. You can bring up your motions relative to that ruling this afternoon if there's a break.

6. We see MR. SAWICKI, film club <u>mentor</u>, and 9 STUDENTS, who are casually dressed.

7. Another of the planners of this crime was to stand outside the drugstore and <u>impede</u> anyone chasing the robbers.

8. Yet another of the <u>conspirators</u>, the planners of this robbery that left a man dead, was to go into the store prior to the robbery to check it out . . . .

9. Even though it was Mr. Nesbitt's gun, it was not Mr. Nesbitt who caused his own death. This was no <u>suicide</u>.

10. You will have the unpleasant task of listening to people who have committed crimes, who have lied and stolen, and in at least one instance has been an admitted, and let me emphasize this, an admitted <u>accomplice</u> to murder.

Monster Vocabulary Worksheet Assignment 1 Continued

Part II: Determining the Meaning -- Match the vocabulary words to their dictionary definitions.

_____ 1. Corridor   A. Block; get in the way of

_____ 2. Obscene   B. Helper in an illegal act

_____ 3. Unshackle   C. Can be allowed in

_____ 4. Counsel   D. Hallway

_____ 5. Admissible   E. Vulgar; offensive; indecent

_____ 6. Mentor   F. Intentionally killing oneself

_____ 7. Impede   G. Attorney

_____ 8. Conspirators   H. Take off chains or restraints

_____ 9. Suicide   I. People who plan an illegal or evil act

_____ 10. Accomplice   J. Trusted advisor or counselor

VOCABULARY ASSIGNMENT 2 *Monster*

Part I: Using Prior Knowledge and Contextual Clues

Below are the sentences in which the vocabulary words appear in the text. Read the sentence. Use any clues you can find in the sentence combined with your prior knowledge, and write what you think the underlined words mean on the lines provided.

1. He is of average height but heavily built with large, <u>ashy</u> hands.

   _____

2. This is a good time for a break. . . . Let's <u>adjourn</u> until tomorrow.

   _____

3. We hear the sounds of fists <u>methodically</u> punching someone as the camera goes slowly down the corridor . . . .

   _____

4. It is night; the lights are out except for dim night-lights placed along the walls. . . . We see two inmates <u>silhouetted</u>, beating a third.

   _____

5. Petrocelli: Detective Karyl, can you describe the scene when you entered the drugstore?
   Karyl: It was pretty <u>gruesome</u>.

   _____

6. CUT TO: INTERIOR: Camera <u>pans</u> down aisles of neighborhood DRUGSTORE.

   _____

7. CUT TO: BLACK-AND-WHITE SHOTS from various angles of body in <u>grotesque</u> position.

   _____

8. Chances are the judge will push for life without <u>parole</u>. . . . he might even go for 25 to life.

   _____

9. It's my understanding that the crime-scene technicians didn't find any fingerprints they could establish as belonging to a <u>perpetrator</u>.

   _____

Monster Vocabulary Worksheet Assignment 2 Continued

Part II: Determining the Meaning -- Match the vocabulary words to their dictionary definitions.

_____ 1. Ashy   A. Bizarre; distorted; incongruous

_____ 2. Adjourn   B. One who commits a crime

_____ 3. Methodically C. Pale; light-colored

_____ 4. Silhouetted   D. Proceeding in a systematic order

_____ 5. Gruesome   E. The release of a prisoner before his term has expired

_____ 6. Pan   F. To suspend proceedings until a later time

_____ 7. Grotesque   G. Outlined or showing dark against light

_____ 8. Parole   H. Horrifying; shocking

_____ 9. Perpetrator   I. Slow, systematic camera movement to show a view of a large area

VOCABULARY ASSIGNMENT 3 *Monster*

Part I: Using Prior Knowledge and Contextual Clues

Below are the sentences in which the vocabulary words appear in the text. Read the sentence. Use any clues you can find in the sentence combined with your prior knowledge, and write what you think the underlined words mean on the lines provided.

1. And how were the <u>proceeds</u> of this robbery going to be divided?

    _____

2. MS of BRIGGS as he walks slowly to the <u>podium</u>.

    _____

3. Mr. Cruz, when you were <u>apprehended</u>, did you make a statement to the police about your part in this crime?

    _____

4. There are tears in his eyes. The pain in his face is very <u>evident</u> as he struggles with his emotions.

    _____

5. . . . we see a crowd in the street below. As camera zooms in, we pick up a <u>cacophony</u> of sounds. Gradually one sound becomes clearer.

    _____

6. He is walking, then trots as the camera pulls back. He is running as camera looks from high angle, and we can no longer <u>distinguish</u> STEVE.

    _____

7. He is a handsome, light-skinned Black who speaks with a <u>precise</u> television-newscaster accent.

    _____

8, 9. They first demanded money and, when the store owner, 55-year-old Alguinaldo Nesbitt was slow in handing over the money, <u>viciously</u> ended his life. Residents of the neighborhood are in absolute <u>dismay</u>. (To neighborhood resident) Sir, can you tell me just how shocked you are by this tragedy?

    _____

    _____

10. Mrs. Harmon: Mrs. Lucas said they got those guys that killed the drugstore owner. . . . She sits down, obviously pleased that the <u>culprits</u> have been caught.

    _____

Monster Vocabulary Worksheet Assignment 3 Continued

Part II: Determining the Meaning -- Match the vocabulary words to their dictionary definitions.

_____ 1. Proceeds   A. Caught

_____ 2. Podium   B. Recognize apart from others

_____ 3. Apprehended   C. People guilty of a crime

_____ 4. Evident   D. Money obtained from a venture

_____ 5. Cacophony   E. Complete loss of courage in the face of trouble or danger

_____ 6. Distinguish   F. Elevated platform for a speaker or conductor

_____ 7. Precise   G. Violently, with mean or evil intent

_____ 8. Viciously   H. Jumbled, discordant sounds

_____ 9. Dismay   I. Clear; obvious; easily seen

_____ 10. Culprits   J. Clearly expressed; distinct and correct in sound or statement

VOCABULARY ASSIGNMENT 4 *Monster*

Part I: Using Prior Knowledge and Contextual Clues

   Below are the sentences in which the vocabulary words appear in the text. Read the sentence. Use any clues you can find in the sentence combined with your prior knowledge, and write what you think the underlined words mean on the lines provided.

1, 2. Forbes: . . . Our records show that Mr. Nesbitt applied for a license to have a gun on the premises in August of 1989. . . .
   VO (Petrocelli): So there was nothing unusual or illegal about the gun being in the drugstore? . . .
   Forbes: Presumably he wanted it for the store. That is correct.

_____

_____

3. The bullet entered the body on the left side and traversed upward through the lung. . . . Death was caused by a combination of trauma to the internal organs, which put the victim into a state of shock, as well as by the lungs filling with blood.

_____

4, 5, 6. She brought me a Bible. The guards had searched it. I wanted to ask if they had found anything in it. Salvation. Grace, maybe. Compassion. She had marked off a passage for me and asked me to read it out loud: "The Lord is my strength and my shield; my heart trusted in him, and I am helped: therefore my heart greatly rejoiceth; and with my song will I praise Him."

_____

_____

_____

7. This phrase is repeated as the camera moves farther and farther away, growing louder and louder as STEVE and KING become tiny figures in the bustling mosaic of Harlem.

_____

Monster Vocabulary Worksheet Assignment 4 Continued

Part II: Determining the Meaning -- Match the vocabulary words to their dictionary definitions.

_____	1.	Premises	A. Wound produced from sudden injury
_____	2.	Presumably	B. Picture or design made up of small pieces
_____	3.	Trauma	C. Mercy or good will of God
_____	4.	Salvation	D. Land and/or buildings
_____	5.	Grace	E. Reasonably assumed
_____	6.	Compassion	F. Deliverance from evil or difficulty
_____	7.	Mosaic	G. Feeling or sharing the suffering of another with the intent of giving aid, support, or showing mercy

VOCABULARY ASSIGNMENT 5 *Monster*

Part I: Using Prior Knowledge and Contextual Clues

Below are the sentences in which the vocabulary words appear in the text. Read the sentence. Use any clues you can find in the sentence combined with your prior knowledge, and write what you think the underlined words mean on the lines provided.

1. She was once a beautiful woman and is still quite attractive, looking far younger than her stated age. She moves with grace to the witness stand . . . .

   _____

2. Mrs. Henry, do you remember an incident that occurred last December in Harlem?

   _____

3. Mrs. Henry, while you were looking over the pictures, were there moments of hesitation? Were there moments when you weren't quite sure, or did you recognize Mr. King as soon as you saw his picture?

   _____

4. Why is he dressed in a prison uniform? The prosecution is going to try to connect him to my client. With him in prison gear, that prejudices my client.

   _____

5, 6. FADE IN: Concentric colorful circles and hurdy-gurdy music: A hustling, bustling cartoon city comes alive on the screen.

   _____

   _____

Monster Vocabulary Worksheet Assignment 5 Continued

Part II: Determining the Meaning -- Match the vocabulary words to their dictionary definitions.

_____ 1.   Grace   A. Event

_____ 2.   Incident   B. Instrument played by turning a crank which causes a resin-covered wheel to scrape across strings

_____ 3.   Hesitation   C. Having a common center

_____ 4.   Prejudices   D. Seemingly effortless beauty or charm in movement

_____ 5.   Concentric   E. Holding back for reason of uncertainty

_____ 6.   Hurdy-gurdy   F. Causes an adverse judgement to be made before the facts are considered

VOCABULARY ASSIGNMENT 6 *Monster*

Part I: Using Prior Knowledge and Contextual Clues

Below are the sentences in which the vocabulary words appear in the text. Read the sentence. Use any clues you can find in the sentence combined with your prior knowledge, and write what you think the underlined words mean on the lines provided.

1, 2. Petrocelli: You really don't know a lot about your cousin, do you?
Moore: I know I saw him that day.
Petrocelli (<u>condescendingly</u>): And what do you do for a living?
Moore: I do a day's work, but I wasn't working that week, because I had hurt my ankle. I went to the doctor that Monday, and you can check that.
Petrocelli: You don't have to <u>verify</u> what you were doing, Mrs. Moore.

_____

_____

3. You're going to have to take the stand–look at the jury and let the jury look at you–and say that you're innocent. I know the judge will tell the jury not to <u>infer</u> anything if you don't take the stand, but I believe that the jury wants to hear from you.

_____

4. You've told me you know King. I don't know why you've chosen this man as an <u>acquaintance</u>, but it's going to hurt you big-time if you don't manage to get some distance between you and him in the eyes of the jury.

_____

5. Briggs: Objection! She knows better than that! . . .
Judge: <u>Sustained.</u> The jury will disregard the last question.

_____

6. He looks out onto the onlookers and sees his parents. His mother forces a smile and his father makes a fist and nods <u>emphatically</u>.

_____

Monster Vocabulary Worksheet Assignment 6 Continued

Part II: Determining the Meaning -- Match the vocabulary words to their dictionary definitions.

_____ 1. Condescendingly   A. Prove the truth of

_____ 2. Verify   B. Person one knows casually

_____ 3. Infer   C. Boldly, definitely, accented

_____ 4. Acquaintance   D. With an air of superiority

_____ 5. Sustained   E. Upheld; supported; maintained

_____ 6. Emphatically   F. Conclude from evidence

VOCABULARY ASSIGNMENT 7 *Monster*

Part I: Using Prior Knowledge and Contextual Clues

Below are the sentences in which the vocabulary words appear in the text. Read the sentence. Use any clues you can find in the sentence combined with your prior knowledge, and write what you think the underlined words mean on the lines provided.

1. We have a man who admits to being part of a robbery accusing another man. And why is he making these <u>accusations</u>?

   _____

2. Isn't the truth of the matter that the only reason he's here is because the police have him on a criminal matter, and have offered him a deal if he comes here and <u>implicates</u> someone else?

   _____

3. All he was supposed to do was to stand outside and push a garbage can in front of a potential <u>pursuer</u>. But there wasn't a <u>pursuer</u>, because Mr. Evans and whoever he was with . . . made sure of that.

   _____

4. I believe justice demands that you reject the testimony of these men, <u>consigning</u> their stories to the area of deep doubt.

   _____

5. The State did <u>elicit</u> from Steve that he spoke to Mr. King about basketball.

   _____

6. They were brought here not to answer for their participation, but for the <u>sole</u> purpose of testifying against others.

   _____

7. But still Mr. Evans goes around selling the cigarettes that connect him with the crime! Did he think that was a clever move? Or is this a shallow, <u>gullible</u> man who doesn't think about very much of anything?

   _____

8, 9, 10. It is about the right we all have to life, liberty, and the pursuit of happiness. It is the <u>contention</u> of the State that no one has the right to <u>deprive</u> us of the <u>precious</u> gift of life.

   _____

   _____

   _____

11. Did she get a break in sentencing? Or was she <u>merely</u> telling the truth?

   _____

Monster Vocabulary Worksheet Assignment 7 Continued

12. . . . are Mr. King or Mr. Evans so accomplished in their criminal activities? This was a <u>botched</u> robbery in which the perpetrators actually took very little money and a few cartons of cigarettes. And, oh, yes, the life of a good man, Alguinaldo Nesbitt.

_____

13. "Steve Harmon made a <u>moral</u> decision," Ms. Petrocelli said.

_____

14. King! Harmon! You got a <u>verdict</u>! Let's go!

_____

15. He has <u>transcribed</u> the images and conversations as he remembers them.

_____

Part II: Determining the Meaning -- Match the vocabulary words to their dictionary definitions.

_____ 1.   Accusations   A. Only; simply

_____ 2.   Implicates   B. Valuable

_____ 3.   Pursuer   C. Bring forth

_____ 4.   Consigning   D. Implies involvement

_____ 5.   Elicit   E. Keep from

_____ 6.   Sole   F. Charges of wrongdoings

_____ 7.   Gullible   G. Ruined through clumsiness

_____ 8.   Contention   H. One who chases after

_____ 9.   Deprive   I. Point put forth in an argument

_____ 10.   Precious   J. Single

_____ 11.   Merely   K. Handing over to permanently

_____ 12.   Botched   L. Easily deceived

_____ 13.   Moral   M. Decision from a jury

_____ 14.   Verdict   N. Written down

_____ 15.   Transcribed   O. Arising from the sense of right and wrong

ANSWER KEY - VOCABULARY
Monster

	1	2	3	4	5	6	7
1	D	C	D	D	D	D	F
2	E	F	F	E	A	A	D
3	H	D	A	A	E	F	H
4	G	G	I	F	F	B	K
5	C	H	H	C	C	E	C
6	J	I	B	G	B	C	J
7	A	A	J	B			L
8	I	E	G				I
9	F	B	E				E
10	B		C				B
11							A
12							G
13							O
14							M
15							N

DAILY LESSONS

LESSON ONE

Objectives
1. To introduce the *Monster* unit
2. To distribute books, study guides and other related materials
3. To preview the vocabulary and study questions for Assignment 1
4. To read Assignment 1

Note: The level of your students will determine how involved you will make this introductory activity. You may want students to simply sketch with their pencils or pens on notebook paper, you may want to have posterboard, markers, and crayons available for real works of art, or you may choose to do something in between. *Tell students in advance if you want them to bring their own materials for this activity. (And be sure to have some extras on hand for students who "forget.")*

Activity #1
Ask students if they have ever dreamed or thought about a monster or monsters. What did they look like? How did they act? Get responses from several students. Tell students to draw the best picture of a monster that they can draw (using whatever materials they have or you have provided). Give students about 15 minutes for this activity.

Activity #2
Have a monster poster show and tell, giving students each a small amount of time to show their drawings. Display the posters in your room (if you can), posting them on the walls or bulletin board(s).

Activity #3
Hold a short discussion about the characteristics of monsters. Write down a list of monster characteristics on the board, and have students write it down, too. (We'll use this list later in the unit when discussing whether or not Steve is a monster.) Ask students whether or not monsters are real. Ask if any people are monster-like. Ask what characteristics would make a real person monster-like.

Transition: Tell students that the book they are going to read is called *Monster*. Explain that it isn't about a monster like the ones they drew, but about people.

Activity #4
Distribute the Theme Project Assignment Sheet and discuss the directions in detail. Themes or ideas to assign:
  human being/monster
  religion
  guilt/innocence
  good/evil
  truth
  point of view

Activity #5
Distribute the materials students will use in this unit. Explain in detail how students are to use these materials.

Study Guides Students should preview the study guide questions before each reading assignment to get a feeling for what events and ideas are important in that section. After reading the section, students will (as a class or individually) answer the questions to review the important events and ideas from that section of the book. Students should keep the study guides as study materials for the unit test. **Give students a few minutes to read through the study questions for the first reading assignment.**

Vocabulary Prior to reading each assignment, students will do vocabulary work related to the section of the book they are about to read. Following the completion of the reading of the book, there will be a vocabulary review of all the words used in the vocabulary assignments. Students should keep their vocabulary work as study materials for the unit test. **Do the first vocabulary worksheet orally with your class to show them how they will do the other vocabulary worksheets in this unit.**

Reading Assignment Sheet You need to fill in the reading assignment sheet to let students know when their reading has to be completed. You can either write the assignment sheet on a side blackboard or bulletin board and leave it there for students to see each day, or you can "ditto" copies for each student to have. In either case, you should advise students to become very familiar with the reading assignments so they know what is expected of them.

Extra Activities Center The Unit Resource Materials portion of this unit contains suggestions for a library of related books and articles in your classroom as well as crossword and word search puzzles. Make an extra activities center in your room where you will keep these materials for students to use. (Bring the books and articles in from the library and keep several copies of the puzzles on hand.) Explain to students that these materials are available for students to use when they finish reading assignments or other class work early.

Nonfiction Assignment Sheet Explain to students that they each are to read at least one non-fiction piece from the in-class library at some time during the unit. Students will fill out a nonfiction assignment sheet after completing the reading to help you evaluate their reading experiences and to help the students think about and evaluate their own reading experiences.

Books Each school has its own rules and regulations regarding student use of school books. Advise students of the procedures that are normal for your school.

Activity#6
Tell students that they should read Assignment #1 prior to the next class period. Give them the remainder of this class (if any time remains) to complete this assignment.

THEME PROJECT ASSIGNMENT - *Monster*

Name _____

Theme Assignment _____

Other Students Assigned This Theme   _____
                                       _____
                                       _____

In *Monster*, there are several ideas or themes that show up throughout the book. You have been assigned one of these ideas or themes for this Theme Project.

Your assignment is to write down any references to it that you can find as you read the book. Use the chart on the following pages to record what you find and any comments/ideas/notes you have about the reference. (Use additional pages if necessary.)

About half-way through reading this book, you and the other students who have been assigned your theme (whose names are listed above) will get together to compare the information you have collected and to talk about what you have found.

When we have completed the reading of the book, you and your theme group members will again meet to compare notes and discuss your findings. At that time, you will prepare to make a brief presentation about your theme to the class.

Your presentation should last no longer than five minutes. In it you should:
   1. State your theme or idea.
   2. Discuss how your theme or idea relates to the book, giving specific examples.
   3. Ask your classmates for any ideas or questions they have about the theme or idea, given the information you have presented.

NOTES FOR THEME ASSIGNMENT
Monster

Theme _____

I Found The Reference While Reading Steve's Entry For This Date:	It Was Located On Page:	The Reference I Found Said This:	Comments/Ideas/Notes:

I Found The Reference While Reading Steve's Entry For This Date:	It Was Located On Page:	The Reference I Found Said This:	Comments/Notes:

LESSON TWO

Objectives:
1. To review the main ideas and events of reading assignment 1
2. To preview the study questions and vocabulary for reading assignment 2
3. To read assignment 2
4. To discuss point of view

Activity #1

Have students answer the study guide questions for reading assignment 1. Allow time for any necessary discussion. Write the correct answers on the board or overhead projector so students can copy them down for study use.

Teacher's Note: Depending on the students' level, different students could write the answers on the board or even ask the questions to lead the group discussion. Jump in as necessary to guide the discussion. Use whatever techniques your particular group will handle best.

Activity #2

Look ahead at the study questions for the second writing assignment with your students. Then, do the vocabulary worksheet for assignment two orally as a class. Make sure students write down the correct answers.

Activity #3

Give each student a copy of the Point Of View Assignment. Discuss the assignment in detail. Give students ample time to complete the assignment, and then have students read their paragraphs aloud. In your discussion of the incident and the different points of view, ask your class to note some of the different points of view Steve incorporates into his film. One of the theme groups has been assigned point of view, but the whole class should take note of this important aspect of the book.(Collect students' paragraphs for grading if you choose, but this is really just an exercise in recognizing that people see the same incident in different ways, depending on their involvement–or lack of involvement–with it, and a way to get students to recognize points of view as they read.)

Activity #4

Tell students that prior to the class meeting after next they should read assignment 2.

POINT OF VIEW ASSIGNMENT
Monster

The following is an account of a crime as written in a police report:

> On August 26th, around 10:15 p.m., an unknown male suspect entered the Franklin Square Market, 4040 West Franklin Boulevard. The suspect placed a gun to the head of a market employee and dragged him to the company's safe. He ordered the employee to empty money from the safe into a bag. The suspect then took the bag and fled on foot.

Your assignment is to write about this incident from the point of view of the person indicated on the list of characters below:

> the market employee
> a woman in the store
> the suspect who robbed the market
> a lookout man working with the suspect
> an older woman in the neighborhood
> a teenager in the neighborhood
> a mother in the neighborhood
> a minister in the neighborhood
> a policeman on the scene just after the robbery
> the spouse of the market employee
> a friend of the suspect who robbed the store
> a judge sentencing the robber
> the mother or father of the robber

How would your character relate the incident, or what would your character have to say about it? Make some notes here, and then write a paragraph or two from your character's point of view.

LESSON THREE

Objectives
    1. To examine some of the film documentary techniques used in *Monster*
    2. To give students the opportunity to work with the techniques discussed
    3. To give students a different perspective on their own lives
    4. To have students practice writing to inform in a format other than an essay

Activity #1
    Tell students to look in their books and follow along as you point out some of the techniques Steve uses in his film making and Walter Dean Myers uses to tell Steve's story in printed form. Some things you'll want to note are:

Myers's use of different typefaces to help distinguish different kinds of information in the book
    For example: a "handwritten" typeface for Steve's personal comments in his journal
                       Capital letters for character names and film directions
                       a small, bold typeface for the stage directions and descriptions
                       a courier typeface for direct speech
                       a unique, bold typeface for words that would appear on the screen in the film

Steve's inclusion of   Fade In/Out
                           Cut To
                           Voice Over (VO)
                           Close Up (CU), Medium Shot (MS), Long Shot (LS)
                           Film Credits
                           Descriptions
                           Stage Directions
                           Flashbacks

Activity #2
    Distribute Writing Assignment #1 and discuss the directions in detail. Talk with your students about this assignment, giving them any additional criteria or information you might require.

WRITING ASSIGNMENT #1
Monster
Writing to Inform

PROMPT
Steve decided to make a film of his experiences. In order to do so, he made notes and wrote a script in his notebook. Through his film, we are informed of the facts of his case as well as his thoughts and feelings about events in his life. Your assignment is to create a script for a film of one day in your life.

PREWRITING
You are receiving this assignment today. Tomorrow you will keep notes in a notebook all day and think about how you can present each part of your day–along with your thoughts, feelings, any appropriate flashbacks, etc. Then, on the next day, in class, you will begin to actually write your script.

Take good notes tomorrow. Get or make a notebook in which you can write down the details of your day. Be observant and be specific about the things you see and do, the people around you, the "scenes" you are part of, etc. Jot down your thoughts as you go through the day, too. These notebooks and the script will not be shared with the class.

DRAFTING
Your first draft will be done in class. When you actually go to write it, first pencil in stage directions and film directions into your notes in your notebook. Do a little editing in your notebook prior to writing your first draft. Read your notes. Pencil through anything that is really not relevant to your day's story. Make some marks blocking out parts of your notes that go together for each "scene" of your day. When you have done these things, go ahead and start writing a draft of your first "scene." Continue for each of the "scenes" in your notes.

When you have completed a draft of each of your "scenes," go back through and read them one after another. Check for continuity and flow. Add any film or stage directions needed. Edit dialogue for clarity.

PROOFREADING
After you have finished a rough draft of your composition, revise it yourself until you are happy with your work. Then, ask a student who sits near you to tell you what he/she likes best about your work, and what things he/she thinks can be improved. Take another look at your script keeping in mind your critic's suggestions, and make the revisions you feel are necessary. Do a final proofreading of your paper double-checking your grammar, spelling, organization, and the clarity of your ideas.

LESSON FOUR

Objectives
1. To review the main ideas and events from reading assignment 2
2. To examine a variety of careers that are available in the criminal justice system and film industry
3. To preview the study questions and do the vocabulary work for reading assignment 3

Activity #1
   Have students answer the study guide questions for reading assignment 2. Allow time for any necessary discussion. Write the correct answers on the board or overhead projector so students can copy them down for study use.

   Teacher's Note: Answering the study questions can be done orally as a class, in small groups with a whole class review following, with student leaders (as in Lesson Two), using the Multiple Choice Study/Quiz questions as quizzes with a whole class review following, or in any way you choose. *In future lessons, the activity will simply say, "Have students answer the study questions for reading assignment __ as directed previously." You can then choose how you would like to do the answers on any given day for any class.*

Activity # 2
   Take a few minutes to preview the study questions for reading assignment 3 with your class.

Activity #3
   Either give students time to complete the vocabulary worksheet for assignment 3 independently, in small groups, or as a class. Discuss or post the answers so all students have the correct answers to study from.

Activity #4
   The remainder of this class period is devoted to exploring careers in the criminal justice system and in the film industry. Introduce this activity by relating it to the book. "In *Monster* we see the criminal justice system in action, and we see some of the process by which a film is made. There are many careers available in both the criminal justice system and in film making." Let students brainstorm careers in these areas. If you choose option 2 below, students may add careers that your class brainstorms to the list provided.
   Choose one of these two ways to explore career opportunities and use your time accordingly:
   1. Invite a guest speaker who is knowledgeable about careers in these two areas–perhaps someone from an employment agency, your school's career counselor, or a career counselor from a local college–to come speak with your students and share information about opportunities in these fields.
   2. Take your students to the library, media center, career office, computer/internet lab, or whatever place in your school will have this information available. Give students the Career Research Guide (on the next page of this manual). Explain that they are to choose one of the careers listed (or that they have added from your class discussion) and complete the required information on the research guide.

CAREER RESEARCH GUIDE
Monster

Choose from one of the following careers:

Criminal Justice System Careers

Airport Security Agent	Homeland Security Agent
ATF Agent	INS Agent
Attorney	Intervention Specialist
Bailiff	Judge
CIA Agent	Juvenile Services Officer
Coast Guard	Paralegal
Compliance Officer	Parole Officer
Corrections Officer	Private Security
Court Reporter	Police Detective
Court Clerk	Police Officer
Crime Scene Investigator	Probation Officer
Criminologist	Private Investigator
Customs Agent	Secret Service Agent
DEA Agent	Sheriff
FBI Agent	US Marshall
Forensic Psychologist	Victim/Witness
Forensic Scientist	Coordinator

Filmmaking Careers

Actor	Grip
Agent	Key Grip
Art Director	Lighting Technician
Assistant Director	Location Manager
Best Boy	Production Assistant
Boom Operator	Production Designer
Camera Operator	Production Sound Mixer
Cinematographer	Property Master
Costume Design	Script Supervisor
Dialogue Editor	Set Decorator
Dolly Grip	Sound Designer
Executive Producer	Sound Editor
Film Director	Special Effects Engineer
Film Producer	Studio Engineer
Focus Puller	Stunt Person
Foley Artist	Video Editor
Gaffer	Writer

Your Name
_____

Career Title

Description Of The Job

Education Required

Expected Current Salary Range

Places Of Employment

Are Jobs Easy Or Hard To Get? Why?

LESSON FIVE

Objectives
1. To complete Writing Assignment #1
2. To read assignment 3

Activity #1

Students have had a whole day to write down their notes in their notebooks. Use this class period for students to complete the assignment and actually write the script. Circulate around the room scanning student work to look for potential problems and to help any students who need guidance.

Activity #2

Students who finish the writing assignment early should start to read assignment 3. This assignment should be completed by all students prior to the next class meeting.

LESSON SIX

Objectives
1. To review the main ideas and events from reading assignment 3
2. To preview the study questions and do the vocabulary work for reading assignment 4
3. To read assignment 4
4. To evaluate students' oral reading

Activity #1

Answer the study questions for reading assignment 3, as directed previously.

Activity #2

Read through the study questions for the 4th reading assignment with your students.

Activity #3

Do the vocabulary worksheet for reading assignment 4 orally with your students. Make sure all students have the correct answers before proceeding with the reading.

Activity #4

Have students read the 4th reading assignment orally in class. There is a Parts Assignment Sheet you can prepare in advance to help you with the part assignments so you don't have to do it on the fly as your students read. (You could also complete this assignment sheet with students' names and give it to them a day or two in advance if you want them to have time to practice their speaking parts.) If you do not finish reading assignment 4 in class, you could continue the oral reading evaluations in Lesson Eight.

READING PART ASSIGNMENT SHEET
Reading Assignment 4
Monster

Character	From These Words	To These Words	Student
Stage/Film Directions	Fade In: Interior: Early morning in Cell Block D . . .	. . . screen goes dark	
Voice-Over	Ain't no use putting the . . .	This is the real deal.	
Stage/Film Directions	VO continues with anonymous prisoner . . .	. . . outfits by the State of New York	
VO	Yo, Harmon, . . .	You want them?	
Steve	All *dialogue* parts by Steve for assignment 4		
Sunset	All *dialogue* parts for Sunset for assignment 4		
Stage/Film Directions	Cut To: Interior: Corrections Dept. Van . . .	She is all business as she talks to Steve	
O'Brien	All *dialogue* parts for O'Brien for assignment 4		
Stage/Film Directions	Cut To: Interior: Holding Room	Kathy O'Brien sits next to Steve	
Stenographer Guard 1 Court Clerk Judge, VO	All *dialogue* parts for these minor characters for assignment 4		
Stage/Film Directions	The Judge enters	Tony sitting on the ground (end of assignment 4)	
Petrocelli	Ready, Your Honor	robbery and the murder, was James King	
Briggs	All *dialogue* parts for Briggs for assignment 4		
Sawicki	All *dialogue* parts for Sawicki for assignment 4		
Petrocelli	Mr. King is the man sitting	caused the death of Alguinaldo Nesbitt. Thank you.	
Jose	All *dialogue* parts for Jose for assignment 4		
Petrocelli	What time did you leave	(end of assignment 4)	
Zinzi	All *dialogue* parts for Zinzi for assignment 4		

ORAL READING EVALUATION *Monster*

Name _____ Class____ Date _____

SKILL	EXCELLENT	GOOD	AVERAGE	FAIR	POOR
Fluency	5	4	3	2	1
Clarity	5	4	3	2	1
Audibility	5	4	3	2	1
Pronunciation	5	4	3	2	1
Portrayal of Character	5	4	3	2	1
_____	5	4	3	2	1

Total _____   Grade _____

Comments:

LESSON SEVEN

Objectives
1. To bring ideas from the book into real life
2. To inform students about the criminal justice system really works

Activity
We have set this day aside for a guest speaker. Invite one or more of the following people from your local criminal justice system to speak to your class:

State's Prosecutor	Corrections Officer	Court Reporter
Judge	Criminal Defense Attorney	Police Officer
Parole Officer	Sheriff (or deputy)	Forensic Scientist

Tell your speakers you want them to tell your class about what they do–what their jobs are, and how they fit into the criminal justice system.

See if you can get one of your speakers to tell students what happens to people when they are arrested–the whole process from the beginning of the arrest through (assuming they're guilty) the end of their prison sentence.

Divide your class time according to how many speakers you're able to acquire, plus allowing time for student questions and responses. Let each person know how long he/she will have to make a presentation to students.

Follow-up: Be sure you and/or your students write a thank you note to each of your guests. At the very least, get a thank you card for each guest and have each of your students sign it (with any personal comments, if there is room).

LESSON EIGHT

Objectives
1. To complete the oral reading evaluations
2. To complete reading assignment 4
3. To review the main ideas and events from assignment 4
4. To review the study questions and do the vocabulary worksheet for assignment 5
5. To read assignment 5

Activity #1
If you did not complete reading assignment 4 in Lesson Six, complete it now.

Activity #2
Have students answer the study questions for assignment 4 as directed previously.

Activity #3
Read through the study questions for assignment 5 with students.

Activity #4
Have students complete the vocabulary worksheet for assignment 5. You may want to do this orally as a class if you want to complete the oral reading evaluations by reading assignment 5 orally in the remainder of this class period. Otherwise, students may work independently or in groups to complete the worksheet. Discuss or post the answers so all students have the correct information to study from.

Activity #5
Have students read assignment 5. If you have not completed the oral reading evaluations, this is a good time to do so. If you have completed them, students may read silently. Tell students this reading assignment must be completed prior to your next class meeting.

LESSON NINE

Objectives
1. To review the main events and ideas from reading assignment 5
2. To preview the study questions and do the vocabulary worksheet for assignment 6
3. To have students meet in their theme groups to compare notes so far
4. To read assignment 6

Activity #1
Have students answer the study questions for reading assignment 5 as previously directed.

Activity #2
While students have their study questions out, review with students the study questions for assignment 6.

Activity #3
Give students about 15 to 20 minutes to get together with their theme/idea groups to compare notes about passages found so far and to discuss how their findings relate to the book.

Activity #4
Tell students they are to complete the prereading vocabulary worksheet for assignment and to read assignment 6 prior to the next class meeting. If time permits, students may begin this assignment in class as they finish their group meetings.

LESSON TEN

Objectives
1. To review the main events and ideas from reading assignment 6
2. To preview the study questions and do the vocabulary worksheet for assignment 7
3. To read assignment 7

Activity #1
Have students answer the study questions for reading assignment 6 as previously directed.

Activity #2
While students have their study questions out, review with students the study questions for assignment 7.

Activity #3
Tell students they are to complete the prereading vocabulary worksheet for assignment and to read assignment 7 prior to the next class meeting. Students may begin this assignment in class.

LESSON ELEVEN

Objectives
    1. To review the main events and ideas from assignment 7
    2. To give students the opportunity to practice writing to persuade
    3. To help students review the events and ideas from the book
    4. To study Steve's character more in depth

Activity #1
    Have students answer the study questions for reading assignment 7 as previously directed.

Activity #2
    Distribute Writing Assignment 2 and discuss the directions in detail. Give students ample time to complete the assignment. Tell them when the assignment will be collected.

NOTE: A writing evaluation form is included after Writing Assignment 2. As you grade the second writing assignments, fill out one of these for each student. Then, as students complete Writing Assignment #3 in Lesson Fifteen, use the evaluation forms as a basis for individual writing conferences for the second writing assignment.

LESSONS TWELVE

Objectives
    1. To have students meet in their theme groups to compare notes
    2. To discuss the novel on a deeper than direct-recall level

Activity #1
    Give students about 15 to 20 minutes to get together with their theme/idea groups to compare notes about passages found and to discuss how their findings relate to the book.

Activity #2
    Choose the questions from the Extra Discussion Questions/Writing Assignments which seem most appropriate for your students. A class discussion of these questions is most effective if students have been given the opportunity to formulate answers to the questions prior to the discussion. To this end, you may either have all the students formulate answers to all the questions, divide your class into groups and assign one or more questions to each group, or you could assign one question to each student in your class. The option you choose will make a difference in the amount of class time needed for this activity.
    After students have had ample time to formulate answers to the questions, begin your class discussion of the questions and the ideas presented by the questions. Be sure students take notes during the discussion so they have information to study for the unit test.

WRITING ASSIGNMENT #2
Monster
Writing to Persuade

PROMPT

Petrocelli calls Steve–and others like him who steal and do not respect other people's rights–monsters. Yet, in the book (written from Steve's point of view) we do not see Steve as a monster. Your assignment is to be Steve and write a letter to Petrocelli convincing her that you are not a monster.

PREWRITING

Make a list of all the things in the book that show Steve as being human, not a monster. Use things that show he has feelings, things that show his actions were not out of disrespect for others' rights, and things that show his participation as innocent or at least benign. After you complete your list, sort through what you have written to choose the best points to make.

DRAFTING

Write an introductory paragraph in which you (Steve) reminds Petrocelli that she called you a monster, what that meant to you, and the fact that you are not really a monster.

In the body of your letter use the examples you jotted down to make convincing points to show Petrocelli that you (Steve) are not a monster. Share your thoughts and feelings as well as the facts to make your arguments more convincing.

In a concluding paragraph, let Petrocelli know that since you are not a monster at all–since you are, in fact, a pretty good guy who just happened to get caught up in something–you should not share the guilt equally with James King.

PROMPT

After you have finished a rough draft of your letter, revise it yourself until you are happy with your work. Then, ask a student who sits near you to read it and tell you what he/she likes best about your work and what things he/she thinks can be improved. Take another look at your letter keeping in mind your critic's suggestions, and make the revisions you feel are necessary.

PROOFREADING

Do a final proofreading of your paper double-checking your grammar, spelling, organization, and the clarity of your ideas.

DUE DATE _____

WRITING EVALUATION FORM - *Monster*

Name _____ Date _____

Writing Assignment #____   Grade _____

Circle One For Each Item:

Introduction	excellent	good	fair	poor
Body Paragraphs	excellent	good	fair	poor
Conclusion	excellent	good	fair	poor
Grammar:	excellent	good	fair	poor (errors noted)
Spelling:	excellent	good	fair	poor (errors noted)
Punctuation:	excellent	good	fair	poor (errors noted)
Legibility:	excellent	good	fair	poor

Strengths:

Weaknesses:

Comments/Suggestions:

LESSON THIRTEEN

Objectives
    1. To discuss the novel on a deeper than direct-recall level
    2. To check the group theme work projects

Activity #1
    Continue with the Extra Discussion Questions/Writing Assignments if you did not have enough time in Lesson 12 to complete this activity.

Activity #2
    Have each theme group make a short presentation about the themes/ideas they were assigned. Allow ample time for class discussion of the information presented. This activity may run into Lesson Fourteen, depending on the length of discussion time allowed.

EXTRA DISCUSSION QUESTIONS/WRITING ASSIGNMENTS
Monster

Interpretive

1. From what point of view is the story told, and why is that important?

2. What is the setting, and what does it add to the story?

3. Based on the facts in the story, can you tell approximately in what decade the story takes place? Does it matter? What things about this book are timeless–true no matter what the year is?

4. Give a character sketch of each of the main characters in the book: Steve Harmon, Sandra Petrocelli, Kathy O'Brien, James King, Richard "Bobo" Evans, Osvaldo Cruz, Lorelle Henry, Jose Delgado, Asa Briggs, and Wendell Bolden.

5. Where were flashbacks used in the book? What did each flashback show?

6. We all have our good points and our bad points. What were Steve's best personality traits? What were his faults?

7. How were the characters who worked at the court and in the jail portrayed? Give specific examples.

Critical

8. Mr. Sawicki said, "When you see a filmmaker getting too fancy, you can bet he's worried either about his story or about his ability to tell it." Relate this to Briggs's defense tactics.

9. Compare and contrast Ernie and Steve (July 11).

10. Compare and contrast Sunset and Steve (July 11).

11. If the story had been written from King's point of view, how would that have changed the story and its effect?

12. Steve repeatedly said, "What did I do?" What DID Steve do?

13. Was Moore a convincing witness? Why or why not?

14. How does the way in which this story is told–as a script interjected with personal comments from Steve and flashbacks–influence our perception of the story?

Monster Extra Discussion Questions page 2

Critical (continued)

15. Is this story in any way about racial prejudice? Does Steve's race make a difference in any way?

16. What, if anything, should we make of the fact that O'Brien did not return Steve's hug?

17. Compare and contrast the way Steve's mother and father responded to him after he was arrested, through the trial, and after the verdict.

18. Why was Jerry included in the book?

19. Why wasn't Bobo on trial? Was that fair?

20. O'Brien tells Steve a little about her life. His response is, "It sounded like a good life even though she said it like it was nothing special." Explain how this section of the book relates to point of view.

Critical/Personal Response

21. In what ways is *Monster* a comment on the American judicial system?

22. It was said that to make an honest film one has to be an honest person. Is Steve honest?

23. Look at the closing arguments by Petrocelli, O'Brien, and Briggs. Whose closing arguments were the best? Why?

24. What was Steve's biggest mistake?

25. Were Steve's parents good parents?

26. Was justice served in the end?

27. Why did Steve participate in the robbery?

Personal Response

28. Did you like this book? Why or why not?

29. Suppose you were Jerry and Steve were your older brother. What would you think of him after this incident?

30. Why is it important to choose your friends and acquaintances carefully?

31. Did Steve really do anything wrong?

Monster Extra Discussion Questions page 3

Quotations

1. When I look into the small rectangle, I see a face looking back at me but I don't recognize it.

2. Sometimes I feel like I have walked into the middle of a movie. It is a strange movie with no plot and no beginning.

3. When you make a film, you leave an impression on the viewers, who serve as a kind of jury for your film. (July 6)

4. But there are also monsters in our communities–people who are willing to steal and to kill, people who disregard the rights of others.(July 6)

5. Bolden: I just wanted to do the right thing. You know, like a good citizen. (July 7)

6. It's funny, but when I'm sitting in the courtroom, I don't feel like I'm involved in the case. It's like the lawyers and the judge and everybody are doing a job that involves me, but I don't have a role. It's only when I go back to the cells that I know I'm involved.(July 8)

7. "It's too late to put up your holy front now," he said. (July 8)

8. When we got in the court, there was a delay because the stenographer had brought the wrong power cord. The court officer was talking about termites. (July 8)

9. 'Cause I'm a human being. I want a life, too! What's wrong with that? (July 8)

10. "All they can do is put me in jail," he said. "They can't touch my soul." (July 9)

11. I wanted to open my shirt and tell her to look into my heart to see who I really was, who the real Steve Harmon was. (July 9)

12. They do things to you in jail. You can't scare somebody with a look in here. (July 9)

13. "This is part of the American judicial system, and we have to respect every part of it." (July 9)

14. Ma'am, it's just routine. Don't worry about it. (July 9)

15. She smiled at me, and I felt embarrassed that a smile should mean so much. (July 11)

16. "You should have said, 'I didn't do it,'" she said. (July 11)

17. And I knew she felt that I didn't do anything wrong. It was me who wasn't sure. It was me who lay on the cot wondering if I was fooling myself. (July 11)

Monster Extra Discussion Questions page 4

Quotations (continued)

18. They left and there was still too much Sunday left in my life. (July 12)

19. Then . . . we got some fried chicken and some wedgies and some sodas. (July 13)

20. I think King was high or he wouldn't have shot the dude. He didn't have to shoot him. He's the cause of me being in this mess. (July 13)

21. The people rest! (July 13)

22. . . . King's lawyer wanted to make sure the jury connected us because I looked like a pretty decent guy. (July 14)

23. We lie to ourselves here. Maybe we are here because we lie to ourselves. (July 14)

24. I didn't say a magic word and turn into somebody different. But here I am, maybe on the verge of losing my life, or the life I used to have. (July 14)

25. Think about all the tomorrows of your life. (July 14)

26. Truth is something you gave up when you were out there on the street.

27. But yes, Mr. Harmon was involved. He made a moral decision to participate in this "getover." (July 14)

28. I know what right is, what truth is. I don't do tightropes, moral or otherwise. (July 17)

29. STEVE spreads his arms to hug O'Brien, but she stiffens and turns to pick up her papers from the table before them. (July 17)

30. What did she see?

LESSON FOURTEEN

Objectives
1. To complete the group theme discussions
2. To have student research and read nonfiction related to the book to help connect the book to real life
3. To broaden students' knowledge about topics related to the book

Activity #1
Complete any discussions unfinished from Lesson Thirteen.

Activity #2
Take students to the library or media center. With students, brainstorm a list of non-fiction topics that could be related to *Monster*. A short list to get you started is below.

Students should choose a nonfiction topic related to *Monster*, read a substantial article related to that topic, and complete the Nonfiction Assignment Sheet for that article. If you have not yet distributed the Nonfiction Assignment Sheets, do so at this time. Students may use magazines, newspapers or the internet as sources.

A Few Suggested Non-Fiction Topics for *Monster*

> Police reports
> Accounts of crimes
> How police departments work
> Kinds of police officers & their duties
> History of a film studio, like Disney or MGM
> Biography of an actor or actress
> Film-making techniques
> Forensic science
> Witness protection program
> How police investigate crime scenes

Activity #3
Bring the class back together and have each student tell what he/she read about.

NOTE: Compiling the Nonfiction Assignment Sheets into a booklet makes a nice follow-up activity and a handy reference for students.

NONFICTION ASSIGNMENT SHEET *Monster*
(To be completed after reading the required nonfiction article)

Name _____ Date _____

Title of Nonfiction Read _____

Written By _____ Publication Date _____

I. Factual Summary: Write a short summary of the piece you read.

II. Vocabulary
     1. With which vocabulary words in the piece did you encounter some degree of difficulty?

     2. How did you resolve your lack of understanding with these words?

III. Interpretation: What was the main point the author wanted you to get from reading his work?

IV. Criticism
     1. With which points of the piece did you agree or find easy to accept? Why?

     2. With which points of the piece did you disagree or find difficult to believe? Why?

V. Personal Response: What do you think about this piece? OR How does this piece influence your ideas?

LESSON FIFTEEN

Objectives:
    1. To bring the book into real life for students
    2. To give students practice expressing their personal opinions
    3. To get students to think about their own lives and their futures

Activity
    Distribute Writing Assignment #3 and discuss the directions in detail. Give students ample time to complete the assignment. Tell them when the assignment will be collected for grading.

NOTE: While students are completing Writing Assignment #3 in class, call individual students to your desk for individual writing conferences based on Writing Assignments 1 and 2.

LESSON SIXTEEN

Objectives
    To review all of the vocabulary work done in this unit

Activity
    Choose one (or more) of the vocabulary review activities listed on the next page(s) and spend your class period as directed in the activity. Some of the materials for these review activities are located in the Extra Activities Packet in this unit.

LESSON SEVENTEEN

Objective:
    To review the main events and ideas of *Monster*

Activity
    Choose one of the review games/activities included in this packet and spend the remainder of your class time as outlined there.

Activity #3
    Remind students of the unit test in the next class meeting. Stress the review of the study guides and their class notes as a last minute, brush-up review.

WRITING ASSIGNMENT #3
Monster
Writing Personal Opinions

PROMPT

Steve wanted to say to his brother, "Think about all the tomorrows of your life." Your assignment is to write a composition in which you tell what you think about all the tomorrows of *your* life.

PREWRITING

Think a minute about Steve and his brother. What do you think Steve meant by his statement? What does, "Think about all the tomorrows of your life" mean to you? Jot down the things it means to you. Taking those things into consideration, think about *your* tomorrows. What do you think about your tomorrows? Jot down your thoughts in words or phrases–or sentences if they come to you that way.

Look over your notes. What things pop out at you as important or meaningful? Is there anything you'd like to add or expand upon?

Arrange your thoughts (your notes) into a logical, coherent sequence.

DRAFTING

Your personal essay should have an introductory paragraph. You may use Steve's quote in the introduction if you wish. Your introduction should make a single statement that covers all of your main thoughts about your tomorrows.

The body of your essay should explain your thoughts about your tomorrows in a logical, coherent sequence. Each paragraph needs a topic sentence and everything in the paragraph should be connected to that topic.

Your composition should have a concluding paragraph so you don't just leave your reader hanging, wondering if there is a page missing or more to come.

PROMPT

After you have finished a rough draft of your composition, revise it yourself until you are happy with your work. Then, ask a student who sits near you to read it and tell you what he/she likes best about your work and what things he/she thinks can be improved. Take another look at your essay keeping in mind your critic's suggestions, and make the revisions you feel are necessary.

PROOFREADING

Do a final proofreading of your paper double-checking your grammar, spelling, organization, and the clarity of your ideas.

DUE DATE _____

VOCABULARY REVIEW ACTIVITIES

1. Divide your class into two teams and have an old-fashioned spelling or definition bee.

2. Give each of your students (or students in groups of two, three or four) a *Monster* Vocabulary Word Search Puzzle. The person (group) to find all of the vocabulary words in the puzzle first wins.

3. Give students a *Monster* Vocabulary Word Search Puzzle without the word list. The person or group to find the most vocabulary words in the puzzle wins.

4. Use a *Monster* Vocabulary Crossword Puzzle. Put the puzzle onto a transparency on the overhead projector (so everyone can see it), and do the puzzle together as a class.

5. Give students a *Monster* Vocabulary Matching Worksheet to do.

6. Divide your class into two teams. Use the *Monster* vocabulary words with their letters jumbled as a word list. Student 1 from Team A faces off against Student 1 from Team B. You write the first jumbled word on the board. The first student (1A or 1B) to unscramble the word wins the chance for his/her team to score points. If 1A wins the jumble, go to student 2A and give him/her a definition. He/she must give you the correct spelling of the vocabulary word which fits that definition. If he/she does, Team A scores a point, and you give student 3A a definition for which you expect a correctly spelled matching vocabulary word. Continue giving Team A definitions until some team member makes an incorrect response. An incorrect response sends the game back to the jumbled-word face off, this time with students 2A and 2B. Instead of repeating giving definitions to the first few students of each team, continue with the student after the one who gave the last incorrect response on the team. For example, if Team B wins the jumbled-word face-off, and student 5B gave the last incorrect answer for Team B, you would start this round of definition questions with student 6B, and so on. The team with the most points wins!

UNIT REVIEW GAMES/ACTIVITIES - *Monster*

1. Ask the class to make up a unit test for *Monster*. The test should have 4 sections: matching, true/false, short answer, and essay. Students may use 1/2 period to make the test and then swap papers and use the other 1/2 class period to take a test a classmate has devised. (open book) You may want to use the unit test included in this packet or take questions from the students' unit tests to formulate your own test.

2. Take 1/2 period for students to make up true and false questions (including the answers). Collect the papers and divide the class into two teams. Draw a big tic-tac-toe board on the chalk board. Make one team X and one team O. Ask questions to each side, giving each student one turn. If the question is answered correctly, that students' team's letter (X or O) is placed in the box. If the answer is incorrect, no mark is placed in the box. The object is to get three marks in a row like tic-tac-toe. You may want to keep track of the number of games won for each team.

3. Take 1/2 period for students to make up questions (true/false and short answer). Collect the questions. Divide the class into two teams. You'll alternate asking questions to individual members of teams A & B (like in a spelling bee). The question keeps going from A to B until it is correctly answered, then a new question is asked. A correct answer does not allow the team to get another question. Correct answers are +2 points; incorrect answers are -1 point.

4. Have students pair up and quiz each other from their study guides and class notes.

5. Give students a *Monster* crossword puzzle to complete.

6. Divide your class into two teams. Use the *Monster* word list words with their letters jumbled as a word list. Student 1 from Team A faces off against Student 1 from Team B. You write the first jumbled word on the board. The first student (1A or 1B) to unscramble the word wins the chance for his/her team to score points. If 1A wins the jumble, go to student 2A and give him/her a clue. He/she must give you the correct word which matches that clue. If he/she does, Team A scores a point, and you give student 3A a clue for which you expect another correct response. Continue giving Team A clues until some team member makes an incorrect response. An incorrect response sends the game back to the jumbled-word face off, this time with students 2A and 2B. Instead of repeating giving clues to the first few students of each team, continue with the student after the one who gave the last incorrect response on the team. For example, if Team B wins the jumbled-word face-off, and student 5B gave the last incorrect answer for Team B, you would start this round of clue questions with student 6B, and so on.

UNIT TESTS

SHORT ANSWER UNIT TEST 1 *Monster*

I. Matching/Identification

____ 1. DIABLOS   A. O'Brien wanted to see Steve's reaction to these she put on the table.

____ 2. PETROCELLI   B. Petrocelli said Steve made a ___ decision to participate in the robbery

____ 3. COLLEGE   C. I wanted to open my shirt and tell her to look into my ____ to see who I really was.

____ 4. ERNIE   D. Gang Osvaldo joined

____ 5. JAIL   E. He didn't think he was guilty because he didn't take anything out of the store.

____ 6. SMILE   F. They take away your shoelaces and this in jail so you can't kill yourself.

____ 7. SOUL   G. He was killed.

____ 8. OBRIEN   H. Prosecutor Sandra

____ 9. ZINZI   I. The murder weapon

____ 10. DO   J. I felt embarrassed that a ___ would mean so much.

____ 11. BOBO   K. Phrase King used regarding the robbery: getting ___

____ 12. BELT   L. Witness who saw King and Bobo in the store

____ 13. NESBITT   M. He called Detective Gluck.

____ 14. HUG   N. Mr. Harmon dreamed Steve would go to ___ and play football

____ 15. GUN   O. Steve's younger brother

____ 16. PAID   P. Steve tries to give one to O'Brien

____ 17. TONY   Q. Richard Evans

____ 18. MORAL   R. Sal got information about the robbery from him.

____ 19. BOLDEN   S. What did I __? What did I __?

____ 20. PICTURES   T. He found the body.

____ 21. JERRY   U. Steve said truth is this.

____ 22. HENRY   V. All they can do is put me in jail. They can't touch my ____.

____ 23. HEART   W. He was beaten up in the park.

____ 24. TRUTH   X. Steve's parents visited him there.

____ 25. JOSE   Y. Defense attorney Kathy

Monster Short Answer Unit Test 1 Page 2

II. Short Answer

1. What does the narrator decide to write in the notebook he is given?

2. What does the narrator name his future film? Why?

3. According to Sandra Petrocelli, who are the monsters in the community?

4. According to Kathy O'Brien, what is the wonder and beauty of the American system of justice?

5. Why does Sal Zinzi call Detective Gluck with a tip about the robbery?

6. How does Steve feel in the courtroom?

7. What is Steve's answer when the older prisoner asks, "Why should you walk?"

8. According to O'Brien, are people innocent until proven guilty?

9. What three of Osvaldo's actions does O'Brien point out to show he is not a fearful person?

10. What is the guard's reaction to Steve's gagging when cleaning the floors?

11. What is Miss O'Brien's response to Steve's telling her he isn't guilty?

12. What reason does Steve give for so many fights in jail?

Monster Short Answer Unit Test 1 Page 3

III. Quotations: Identify the importance of **5** of the following quotes in the book.

1. I just wanted to do the right thing. You know, like a good citizen.

2. 'Cause I'm a human being. I want a life, too! What's wrong with that?

3. You should have said, "I didn't do it," she said.

4. They left and there was still too much Sunday left in my life.

5. Then . . . we got some fried chicken and some wedgies and some sodas.

6. I know what right is, what truth is. I don't do tightropes, moral or otherwise.

7. And I knew she felt that I didn't do anything wrong. It was me who wasn't sure. It was me who lay on the cot wondering if I was fooling myself.

Monster Short Answer Unit Test 1 Page 4

IV. Vocabulary

Write the vocabulary words you are given. After writing them down, go back and write in their definitions.

Word	Definition
1	
2	
3	
4	
5	
6	
7	
8	
9	
10	

ANSWER KEY SHORT ANSWER UNIT TEST 1 *Monster*

I. Matching/Identification

D	1. DIABLOS	A.	O'Brien wanted to see Steve's reaction to these she put on the table.
H	2. PETROCELLI	B.	Petrocelli said Steve made a ___ decision to participate in the robbery
N	3. COLLEGE	C.	I wanted to open my shirt and tell her to look into my ___ to see who I really was.
E	4. ERNIE	D.	Gang Osvaldo joined
X	5. JAIL	E.	He didn't think he was guilty because he didn't take anything out of the store.
J	6. SMILE	F.	They take away your shoelaces and this in jail so you can't kill yourself.
V	7. SOUL	G.	He was killed.
Y	8. OBRIEN	H.	Prosecutor Sandra
M	9. ZINZI	I.	The murder weapon
S	10. DO	J.	I felt embarrassed that a ___ would mean so much.
Q	11. BOBO	K.	Phrase King used regarding the robbery: getting ___
F	12. BELT	L.	Witness who saw King and Bobo in the store
G	13. NESBITT	M.	He called Detective Gluck.
P	14. HUG	N.	Mr. Harmon dreamed Steve would go to ___ and play football
I	15. GUN	O.	Steve's younger brother
K	16. PAID	P.	Steve tries to give one to O'Brien
W	17. TONY	Q.	Richard Evans
B	18. MORAL	R.	Sal got information about the robbery from him.
R	19. BOLDEN	S.	What did I __? What did I __?
A	20. PICTURES	T.	He found the body.
O	21. JERRY	U.	Steve said truth is this.
L	22. HENRY	V.	All they can do is put me in jail. They can't touch my ___.
C	23. HEART	W.	He was beaten up in the park.
U	24. TRUTH	X.	Steve's parents visited him there.
T	25. JOSE	Y.	Defense attorney Kathy

Monster Short Answer Unit Test 1 Answer Key Page 2

II. Short Answer

1. What does the narrator decide to write in the notebook he is given?
    He decides to write down the story of this experience as a film.

2. What does the narrator name his future film? Why?
    He calls it "Monster" because that's what the lady prosecutor called him.

3. According to Sandra Petrocelli, who are the monsters in the community?
    People who are willing to steal and to kill, people who disregard the rights of others, are monsters.

4. According to Kathy O'Brien, what is the wonder and beauty of the American system of justice?
    The wonder and beauty of the system is that it protects citizens but also the accused.

5. Why does Sal Zinzi call Detective Gluck with a tip about the robbery?
    He wants a break on his jail time in return for the information.

6. How does Steve feel in the courtroom?
    He feels like he is not involved with the case–the judge and lawyers and everyone else are doing everything; he does not have an active part.

7. What is Steve's answer when the older prisoner asks, "Why should you walk?"
    Steve says, "Cause I'm a human being. I want a life, too! What's wrong with that?"

8. According to O'Brien, are people innocent until proven guilty?
    She says it depends on how the jury sees the case.

9. What three of Osvaldo's actions does O'Brien point out to show he is not a fearful person?
    She points out that he fought a member of the Diablos gang and cut a stranger in the face to get into the Diablos gang, and he beat up his girlfriend.

10. What is the guard's reaction to Steve's gagging when cleaning the floors?
    He said, "You vomit–you just got more to clean up!"

11. What is Miss O'Brien's response to Steve's telling her he isn't guilty?
    She said he should have said, "I didn't do it."

12. What reason does Steve give for so many fights in jail?
    He says, "In here all you have going for you is the little surface stuff. . . . you have to protect that."

Monster Short Answer Unit Test 1 Answer Key Page 3

III. Quotations: Identify the importance of **5** of the following quotes in the book.

1. I just wanted to do the right thing. You know, like a good citizen.
    Bolden was testifying as to why he implicated James King in the robbery. Briggs is trying to make the jury believe Bolden just picked out a person at random to get his jail term reduced. Bolden is trying to make himself look good to the jury by portraying himself as a good citizen, skirting the truth of the matter.

2. 'Cause I'm a human being. I want a life, too! What's wrong with that?
    An older prisoner has asked Steve why he should walk. Steve's answer clearly shows he does not believe he has done anything wrong; he is not a monster. He believes he is a decent guy who deserves a life outside of prison.

3. You should have said, "I didn't do it," she said.
    Steve has just told O'Brien that he isn't guilty. This is her response, clearly showing she does believe he did it and IS guilty.

4. They left and there was still too much Sunday left in my life.
    Steve's days are long when there isn't any court or anything going on, but this also has a double meaning within the religious themes in the book. This quote combined with Steve's wanting to tell his brother that his heart was not greatly rejoicing and he was not singing praises indicates that he isn't very religious at all. Perhaps religion makes him feel guilty, makes him feel like a monster–at a time when he sees his life and actions through rose-colored glasses, a time when he is holding on to his innocence and value as a human being.

5. Then . . . we got some fried chicken and some wedgies and some sodas.
    King and Bobo went for lunch after the robbery and murder. This action shows us that committing the crimes didn't bother them at all; it was just another thing in their day.

6. I know what right is, what truth is. I don't do tightropes, moral or otherwise.
    The prosecution's contention was that Steve walked a moral tightrope, trying to act as if what he did wasn't what it seemed, that he didn't *really* DO anything wrong. The prosecution sees him as a willing participant, making him as guilty as King. Steve, on the other hand, tries to convince himself that he only walked around in a store and left, doing nothing wrong. He keeps saying he knows what is right and what truth is–but because he says it over and over, it's more like he's trying to convince himself. It bothers him; he has doubts inside.

7. And I knew she felt that I didn't do anything wrong. It was me who wasn't sure. It was me who lay on the cot wondering if I was fooling myself.
    He IS fooling himself; although he repeatedly says he knows what is right and what truth is, he always has a nagging conscience making him feel uneasy.

Monster Short Answer Unit Test 1 Answer Key Page 4

IV. Vocabulary

Write the vocabulary words you have chosen to test.

Word	Definition
1	
2	
3	
4	
5	
6	
7	
8	
9	
10	

SHORT ANSWER UNIT TEST 2 *Monster*

I. Matching/Identification

____ 1. JOSE   A. Jerry wanted Steve to be this superhero.

____ 2. BOBO   B. Petrocelli said Steve made a ___ decision to participate in the robbery

____ 3. KIDS   C. Mr. Harmon dreamed Steve would go to ___ and play football.

____ 4. STEVE   D. Steve's last name

____ 5. SAWICKI   E. Witness who saw King and Bobo in the store

____ 6. ERNIE   F. I wanted to open my shirt and tell her to look into my ___ to see who I really was.

____ 7. PICTURES   G. Film club sponsor; character witness for Steve

____ 8. NOTEBOOK   H. Twelve people who decide the verdict

____ 9. DIABLOS   I. Steve's younger brother

____ 10. NESBITT   J. Narrator on trial for murder

____ 11. TONY   K. Gang Osvaldo joined

____ 12. LIE   L. Prosecutor Sandra

____ 13. BATMAN   M. He found the body.

____ 14. HUG   N. Richard Evans

____ 15. JERRY   O. Mama brought this book to Steve.

____ 16. HEART   P. Steve wrote his script and notes in it.

____ 17. JURY   Q. He was beaten up in the park.

____ 18. HARMON   R. What did I __? What did I __?

____ 19. COLLEGE   S. Defense attorney Kathy

____ 20. HENRY   T. Maybe we are here because we ___ to ourselves.

____ 21. OBRIEN   U. O'Brien wanted to see Steve's reaction to these she put on the table.

____ 22. BIBLE   V. Steve tries to give one to O'Brien

____ 23. DO   W. He was killed.

____ 24. MORAL   X. They were not allowed in the visitor's area.

____ 25. PETROCELLI Y. He didn't think he was guilty because he didn't take anything out of the store.

Monster Short Answer Unit Test 2 Page 2

II. Short Answer

1. What three of Osvaldo's actions does O'Brien point out to show he is not a fearful person?

2. What is the guard's reaction to Steve's gagging when cleaning the floors?

3. Describe Steve's reaction to Dr. Moody's testimony about how Mr. Nesbitt actually died. What was James King's reaction to it?

4. According to Bobo, was the shooting of Mr. Nesbitt accidental?

5. Steve says, "Maybe we are here _____."

6. Why does O'Brien decide Steve should testify?

7. Why couldn't King testify?

8. Does Steve tell the truth on the witness stand?

9. List **three** of the main points Briggs makes in his closing arguments to the jury.

Monster Short Answer Unit Test 2 Page 3

10. List **three** main points O'Brien makes in her final arguments to the jury.

11. What reason does Petrocelli give the jury to urge them to convict Steve Harmon?

12. What is O'Brien's reaction to Steve's open arms to give her a hug?

13. What is the last image of Steve in the film?

14. What final question is Steve trying to answer?

Monster Short Answer Unit Test 2 Page 4

III. Composition

Was Steve Harmon a monster? Answer in a complete essay using information from the book to support your statements.

Monster Short Answer Unit Test 2 Page 5

IV. Vocabulary

____ 1. PURSUER A. Upheld; supported; maintained

____ 2. SILHOUETTED B. Helper in an illegal act

____ 3. CONSIGNING C. Land and/or buildings

____ 4. CACOPHONY D. Prove the truth of

____ 5. MERELY E. Slow, systematic camera movement to show a large vies

____ 6. SUSTAINED F. Event

____ 7. CULPRITS G. Written down

____ 8. INCIDENT H. Recognize apart from others

____ 9. ACQUAINTANCE I. Implies involvement

____ 10. CONTENTION J. Jumbled, discordant sounds

____ 11. IMPLICATES K. Causes an adverse judgement to be made before facts are considered

____ 12. DISTINGUISH L. Arising from the sense of right and wrong

____ 13. PREJUDICES M. Hallway

____ 14. CORRIDOR N. Permanently handing over to

____ 15. APPREHENDED O. Person one knows casually

____ 16. COMPASSION P. Mercy or good will of God

____ 17. VERIFY Q. Caught

____ 18. PREMISES R. One who chases after

____ 19. MORAL S. Only; simply

____ 20. TRANSCRIBED T. People who plan an illegal or evil act

____ 21. CONSPIRATORS U. Feeling or sharing the suffering of another in the intent of giving aid, support, or showing mercy

____ 22. MENTOR V. Point put forth in an argument

____ 23. GRACE W. People guilty of a crime

____ 24. PAN X. Outlined or showing dark against light

____ 25. ACCOMPLICE Y. Trusted advisor or counselor

ANSWER KEY SHORT ANSWER UNIT TEST 2 *Monster*

I. Matching/Identification

M	1. JOSE	A. Jerry wanted Steve to be this superhero.
N	2. BOBO	B. Petrocelli said Steve made a ___ decision to participate in the robbery
X	3. KIDS	C. Mr. Harmon dreamed Steve would go to ___ and play football.
J	4. STEVE	D. Steve's last name
G	5. SAWICKI	E. Witness who saw King and Bobo in the store
Y	6. ERNIE	F. I wanted to open my shirt and tell her to look into my ___ to see who I really was.
U	7. PICTURES	G. Film club sponsor; character witness for Steve
P	8. NOTEBOOK	H. Twelve people who decide the verdict
K	9. DIABLOS	I. Steve's younger brother
W	10. NESBITT	J. Narrator on trial for murder
Q	11. TONY	K. Gang Osvaldo joined
T	12. LIE	L. Prosecutor Sandra
A	13. BATMAN	M. He found the body.
V	14. HUG	N. Richard Evans
I	15. JERRY	O. Mama brought this book to Steve.
F	16. HEART	P. Steve wrote his script and notes in it.
H	17. JURY	Q. He was beaten up in the park.
D	18. HARMON	R. What did I __? What did I __?
C	19. COLLEGE	S. Defense attorney Kathy
E	20. HENRY	T. Maybe we are here because we ___ to ourselves.
S	21. OBRIEN	U. O'Brien wanted to see Steve's reaction to these she put on the table.
O	22. BIBLE	V. Steve tries to give one to O'Brien
R	23. DO	W. He was killed.
B	24. MORAL	X. They were not allowed in the visitor's area.
L	25. PETROCELLI	Y. He didn't think he was guilty because he didn't take anything out of the store.

Monster Short Answer Unit Test 2 Answer Key Page 2

II. Short Answer

1. What three of Osvaldo's actions does O'Brien point out to show he is not a fearful person?
    She points out that he fought a member of the Diablos gang and cut a stranger in the face to get into the Diablos gang, and he beat up his girlfriend.

2. What is the guard's reaction to Steve's gagging when cleaning the floors?
    He said, "You vomit–you just got more to clean up!"

3. Describe Steve's reaction to Dr. Moody's testimony about how Mr. Nesbitt actually died. What was James King's reaction to it?
    Steve catches his breath sharply. King listens to it without any sign of caring.

4. According to Bobo, was the shooting of Mr. Nesbitt accidental?
    No, it wasn't. King said he "had to light him up because he was trying to muscle him."

5. Steve says, "Maybe we are here _____."
    Maybe we are here because we lie to ourselves."

6. Why does O'Brien decide Steve should testify?
    She wants to put as much distance between Steve and King as possible, and to present Steve as someone the jurors can believe in.

7. Why couldn't King testify?
    The prosecution "can use his own statements against him, and he's cooked."

8. Does Steve tell the truth on the witness stand?
    No, he doesn't.

9. List **three** of the main points Briggs makes in his closing arguments to the jury.
    Any of these answers are correct:
    - Bobo implicates King because the police have him on a criminal matter and have offered him a deal if he comes here and implicates someone else.
    - Bobo's character is that of a criminal, a drug dealer, and a robber.
    - The prosecution did not produce any witnesses to the murder.
    - Mrs. Henry's mind was on her granddaughter; she could have been mistaken about King's identity.
    - Mrs. Moore said King was at her house at the time of the robbery. We can't assume everyone related to the accused would lie.
    - This case is about whether or not you believe people who are admitted participants in this crime and who are saving their own hides. If you believe that their positions, their stated characters, so taint their testimony that everything they say is well within the area of reasonable doubt, then you have no choice but to find Mr. King not guilty.

Monster Short Answer Unit Test 2 Answer Key Page 3

10. List **three** main points O'Brien makes in her final arguments to the jury.
    - The State did not establish any conversation about the robbery between Mr. Harmon and anyone else involved.
    - The State did not even suggest that Mr. Harmon was in the store at the time of the robbery.
    - Mr. Harmon was not with Bobo and King eating chicken after the crime.
    - Mr. Harmon did not receive any of the loot.
    - Mr. Evans and Mr. Cruz implicate Mr. Harmon out of self-interest, to get reduced sentences.
    - To Mr. Evans, Mr. Nesbitt was just a "get over," and that's what Steve is to him, too.
    - Mr. Harmon answered questions openly and honestly on the stand and is of a much better character than the others who took the stand.
    - Mrs. Henry did not identify Steve as being in the store.

11. What reason does Petrocelli give the jury to urge them to convict Steve Harmon?
    "Steve Harmon was part of the plan that caused the death of Alguinaldo Nesbitt. . . . He made a moral decision to participate in this "getover." He wanted to "get paid" with everybody else. He is as guilty as everybody else, no matter how many moral hairs he can split. His participation made the crime easier. His willingness to check out the store, no matter how poorly he did it, was one of those causative factors that resulted in the death of Mr. Nesbitt.

12. What is O'Brien's reaction to Steve's open arms to give her a hug?
    She stiffens and turns to pick up papers on the table.

13. What is the last image of Steve in the film?
    He turns towards the camera with outstretched arms. The picture turns black and white and grainy/distorted. He looks like a monster.

14. What final question is Steve trying to answer?
    What did Miss O'Brien see that caused her to turn away from him at the end of the trial?

III. Composition
    Was Steve Harmon a monster?
    Grade the essays according to your own criteria.

Monster Short Answer Unit Test 2 Answer Key Page 4

IV. Vocabulary

R	1. PURSUER	A. Upheld; supported; maintained
X	2. SILHOUETTED	B. Helper in an illegal act
N	3. CONSIGNING	C. Land and/or buildings
J	4. CACOPHONY	D. Prove the truth of
S	5. MERELY	E. Slow, systematic camera movement to show a large vies
A	6. SUSTAINED	F. Event
W	7. CULPRITS	G. Written down
F	8. INCIDENT	H. Recognize apart from others
O	9. ACQUAINTANCE	I. Implies involvement
V	10. CONTENTION	J. Jumbled, discordant sounds
I	11. IMPLICATES	K. Causes an adverse judgement to be made before facts are considered
H	12. DISTINGUISH	L. Arising from the sense of right and wrong
K	13. PREJUDICES	M. Hallway
M	14. CORRIDOR	N. Permanently handing over to
Q	15. APPREHENDED	O. Person one knows casually
U	16. COMPASSION	P. Mercy or good will of God
D	17. VERIFY	Q. Caught
C	18. PREMISES	R. One who chases after
L	19. MORAL	S. Only; simply
G	20. TRANSCRIBED	T. People who plan an illegal or evil act
T	21. CONSPIRATORS	U. Feeling or sharing the suffering of another in the intent of giving aid, support, or showing mercy
Y	22. MENTOR	V. Point put forth in an argument
P	23. GRACE	W. People guilty of a crime
E	24. PAN	X. Outlined or showing dark against light
B	25. ACCOMPLICE	Y. Trusted advisor or counselor

ADVANCED SHORT ANSWER UNIT TEST *Monster*

I. Matching

____ 1. JOSE   A. Jerry wanted Steve to be this superhero.

____ 2. BOBO   B. Petrocelli said Steve made a ___ decision to participate in the robbery

____ 3. KIDS   C. Mr. Harmon dreamed Steve would go to ___ and play football.

____ 4. STEVE   D. Steve's last name

____ 5. SAWICKI   E. Witness who saw King and Bobo in the store

____ 6. ERNIE   F. I wanted to open my shirt and tell her to look into my ___ to see who I really was.

____ 7. PICTURES   G. Film club sponsor; character witness for Steve

____ 8. NOTEBOOK   H. Twelve people who decide the verdict

____ 9. DIABLOS   I. Steve's younger brother

____ 10. NESBITT   J. Narrator on trial for murder

____ 11. TONY   K. Gang Osvaldo joined

____ 12. LIE   L. Prosecutor Sandra

____ 13. BATMAN   M. He found the body.

____ 14. HUG   N. Richard Evans

____ 15. JERRY   O. Mama brought this book to Steve.

____ 16. HEART   P. Steve wrote his script and notes in it.

____ 17. JURY   Q. He was beaten up in the park.

____ 18. HARMON   R. What did I __? What did I __?

____ 19. COLLEGE   S. Defense attorney Kathy

____ 20. HENRY   T. Maybe we are here because we ___ to ourselves.

____ 21. OBRIEN   U. O'Brien wanted to see Steve's reaction to these she put on the table.

____ 22. BIBLE   V. Steve tries to give one to O'Brien

____ 23. DO   W. He was killed.

____ 24. MORAL   X. They were not allowed in the visitor's area.

____ 25. PETROCELLI   Y. He didn't think he was guilty because he didn't take anything out of the store.

Monster Advanced Short Answer Unit Test Page 2

II. Short Answer

1. Does Steve Harmon know what the truth is? Support your answer.

2. Mr. Sawicki said, "When you see a filmmaker getting too fancy, you can bet he's worried either about his story or about his ability to tell it." Relate this to Briggs's defense tactics.

3. What, if anything, should me make of the fact that O'Brien did not return Steve's hug?

4. Compare and contrast the way Steve's mother and father reacted to him during the trial and afterwards. Who do you think was right? Support your answer.

5. Was justice served in the end? Support your answer.

Monster Advanced Short Answer Unit Test Page 3

III. Composition

Mr. Sawicki said, "When you make a film, you leave an impression on the viewers, who serve as a kind of jury for your film."

You have "seen" Steve Harmon's film. You are its judge and jury. Tell what this "film" is *really* about. Don't just give a plot summary. What is it about in terms of themes and ideas? Write a complete essay and support your ideas with information from the book.

Monster Advanced Short Answer Unit Test Page 4

IV. Vocabulary

    Write down the vocabulary words given, then write a paragraph or two about *Monster* correctly using all of the words.

MULTIPLE CHOICE UNIT TEST 1 *Monster*

I. Matching

____ 1. STEVE   A. He called Detective Gluck.

____ 2. MYERS   B. Ma'am, it's just routine. Don't ___ about it.

____ 3. KING   C. Steve wrote his script and notes in it.

____ 4. SMILE   D. They were not allowed in the visitor's area.

____ 5. BOBO   E. Detective who wanted the death penalty

____ 6. TONY   F. Defense attorney Kathy

____ 7. GUILTY   G. Steve tries to give one to O'Brien

____ 8. BATMAN   H. All they can do is put me in jail. They can't touch my ___.

____ 9. HUG   I. Narrator on trial for murder

____ 10. OBRIEN   J. She testified that King was at her house.

____ 11. TOMORROWS   K. Author Walter Dean

____ 12. NOTEBOOK   L. They take away your shoelaces and this in jail so you can't kill yourself.

____ 13. MOORE   M. Think about all the ___ of your life.

____ 14. BELT   N. Jury's verdict for King

____ 15. JERRY   O. Twelve people who decide the verdict

____ 16. BIBLE   P. Richard Evans

____ 17. SOUL   Q. Maybe we are here because we ___ to ourselves.

____ 18. DIABLOS   R. Gang Osvaldo joined

____ 19. LIE   S. Steve said truth is this.

____ 20. ZINZI   T. He was on trial with Steve.

____ 21. TRUTH   U. Mama brought this book to Steve.

____ 22. KARYL   V. He was beaten up in the park.

____ 23. KIDS   W. I felt embarrassed that a ___ would mean so much.

____ 24. JURY   X. Steve's younger brother

____ 25. WORRY   Y. Jerry wanted Steve to be this superhero.

Monster Multiple Choice Unit Test 1 Page 2

II. Multiple Choice

1. What does the narrator decide to write in the notebook he is given?
    A. He decides to write down the story of this experience as a film.
    B. He decides to write down a mark for each day he is in jail.
    C. He decides to write down his regrets.
    D. He decides to write down letters to his family.

2. What does the narrator name his future film? Why?
    A. He calls it "Monster" because the events are so distorted as he thinks about them.
    B. He calls it "Monster" because he feels like a monster.
    C. He calls it "Monster" because he feels surrounded by monsters in jail.
    D. He calls it "Monster" because that's what the lady prosecutor called him.

3. According to Sandra Petrocelli, who are the monsters in the community?
    A. Defense attorneys who try to keep murderers out of jail.
    B. People who are prejudiced.
    C. People who are willing to steal and to kill; people who disregard the rights of others.
    D. People who don't bother to see others for who they really are.

4. According to Kathy O'Brien, what is the wonder and beauty of the American system of justice?
    A. It always manages to punish the guilty and set innocent people free.
    B. It usually surpasses her lofty expectations.
    C. It dispenses equal justice for all.
    D. It protects citizens but also the accused.

5. Why does Sal Zinzi call Detective Gluck with a tip about the robbery?
    A. He owes Gluck a favor for previously getting his jail time reduced.
    B. He wants to get even with James King by ratting him out to the police.
    C. He wants a break on his jail time in return for the information.
    D. He is hoping for a part of the reward money.

6. How does Steve feel in the courtroom?
    A. He feels uncomfortable because everyone keeps looking at him like he's guilty.
    B. He feels like he is not involved with the case–the judge and lawyers and everyone else are doing everything; he does not have an active part.
    C. He feels like he can't breathe; like all the walls are closing in on him.
    D. He feels like the prosecutor and O'Brien have already cut a deal between themselves and they are just going through the motions of a trial, already knowing the outcome will be a guilty verdict.

Monster Multiple Choice Unit Test 1 Page 3

7. What is Steve's answer when the older prisoner asks, "Why should you walk?"
   A. Steve says, "'Cause I didn't do it!"
   B. Steve says, "'Cause I'm a human being. I want a life, too! What's wrong with that?"
   C. Steve says, "Why shouldn't I? I'm as good as the next guy. Everybody messes up sometime, sooner or later."
   D. Steve says, "I'm not like the others! I never been in trouble before."

8. According to O'Brien, are people innocent until proven guilty?
   A. She says people ARE innocent until proven guilty; that's the hallmark of our system.
   B. She says she never met a defendant who didn't do what they were accused of doing. The guilty get prosecuted; the innocent never get arrested.
   C. She says that's just a dusty old phrase that no one ever pays attention to anymore.
   D. She says it depends on how the jury sees the case.

9. Which of these is NOT one of Osvaldo's actions that O'Brien points out to show he is not a fearful person?
   A. He beat up Tony in the park.
   B. He cut a stranger in the face.
   C. He fought a member of the Diablos gang.
   D. He beat up his girlfriend.

10. What is the guard's reaction to Steve's gagging when cleaning the floors?
    A. He laughed at Steve.
    B. He started gagging, too, and vomited on the floor.
    C. He said, "You vomit–you just got more to clean up!"
    D. He said, "What a pansy! Not even man enough to clean a floor without gagging!"

11. What is Miss O'Brien's response to Steve's telling her he isn't guilty?
    A. She tells him she doesn't believe him, that he is, in fact, a monster.
    B. She turns away in silence.
    C. She says he should have said, "I didn't do it."
    D. She heaves a sigh of relief because it confirms what she has thought all along.

12. What reason does Steve give for so many fights in jail?
    A. He says, "Everyone is so close together, so in each other's faces. It makes everyone edgy. It just has to come out somewhere.
    B. He says, "In here all you have going for you is the little surface stuff. . . . you have to protect that."
    C. He says, "Guys in here have lost everything. Family. Friends. Hope. When there's nothing left in life, there's nothing left but the physical, the fight, the survival."
    D. He says, "Anger builds up. You're angry at being forced into doing something you didn't want to do. And angry that you got caught. And angry that people who aren't like you, in here, don't even look at you anymore. And you're angry at yourself."

Monster Multiple Choice Unit Test 1 Page 4

III. Quotations

Match the beginning of the quote with the ending

___ 1. Sometimes I feel like I have walked into the middle of a movie.

___ 2. I just wanted to do the right thing.

___ 3. All they can do is put me in jail

___ 4. And I knew she felt that I didn't do anything wrong.

___ 5. When I look into the small rectangle,

___ 6. We lie to ourselves here.

___ 7. They left

___ 8. I know what right is, what truth is.

- -

A. And there was still too much Sunday left in my life.

B. It is a strange movie with no plot and no beginning.

C. They can't touch my soul.

D. Maybe we are here because we lie to ourselves.

E. I don't do tightropes, moral or otherwise.

F. You know, like a good citizen.

G. It was me who wasn't sure. It was me who lay on the cot wondering if I was fooling myself.

H. I see a face looking back at me but I don't recognize it.

I. But here I am, maybe on the verge of losing my life, or the life I used to have.

J. I wanted to open my shirt and tell her to look into my heart to see who I really was.

Monster Multiple Choice Unit Test 1 Page 5

IV. Vocabulary

____ 1. VICIOUSLY   A. People guilty of a crime

____ 2. CONCENTRIC   B. Conclude from evidence

____ 3. PREMISES   C. Point put forth in an argument

____ 4. GRACE   D. Mercy or good will of God

____ 5. PAROLE   E. Boldly; definitely; accented

____ 6. SOLE   F. Intentionally killing oneself

____ 7. PRECISE   G. Single

____ 8. MERELY   H. People who plan an illegal or evil act

____ 9. CORRIDOR   I. The release of a prisoner before his term has expired

____10. SILHOUETTED   J. Clear; obvious; easily seen

____11. EVIDENT   K. Outlined or showing dark against light

____12. TRAUMA   L. Having a common center

____13. DISTINGUISH   M. Only; simply

____14. SUSTAINED   N. Keep from

____15. ACCOMPLICE   O. Land and/or buildings

____16. EMPHATICALLY   P. Charges of wrongdoings

____17. SUICIDE   Q. Clearly expressed; distinct and correct in sound or statement

____18. CONTENTION   R. Helper in an illegal act

____19. CONSPIRATORS   S. Wound produced from sudden injury

____20. GRUESOME   T. Decision from a jury

____21. VERDICT   U. Violently with mean or evil intent

____22. DEPRIVE   V. Hallway

____23. INFER   W. Recognize apart from others

____24. CULPRITS   X. Horrifying; shocking

____25. ACCUSATIONS   Y. Upheld; supported; maintained

V. Essay

Show how Walter Dean Myers uses point of view in *Monster* to explore the question, "What is truth?". Use information from the book to support your statements.

MULTIPLE CHOICE UNIT TEST 2 *Monster*

I. Matching

____ 1. JERRY   A. Steve's job in the robbery

____ 2. KIDS   B. Gang Osvaldo joined

____ 3. LOOKOUT   C. Witnesses do this in court.

____ 4. PETROCELLI   D. Narrator on trial for murder

____ 5. KARYL   E. Steve's younger brother

____ 6. GUILTY   F. Detective who wanted the death penalty

____ 7. WORRY   G. He was to detain anyone chasing the robbers.

____ 8. STEVE   H. O'Brien wanted to see Steve's reaction to these she put on the table.

____ 9. BIBLE   I. Twelve people who decide the verdict

____ 10. MONSTER   J. All they can do is put me in jail. They can't touch my ____.

____ 11. SAWICKI   K. Petrocelli said Steve made a ____ decision to participate in the robbery

____ 12. LIE   L. Maybe we are here because we ____ to ourselves.

____ 13. JURY   M. I wanted to open my shirt and tell her to look into my ____ to see who I really was.

____ 14. PICTURES   N. Jerry wanted Steve to be this superhero.

____ 15. DIABLOS   O. Steve looks like one at the end of the film.

____ 16. BATMAN   P. Film club sponsor; character witness for Steve

____ 17. HENRY   Q. Mama brought this book to Steve.

____ 18. COLLEGE   R. Jury's verdict for King

____ 19. SOUL   S. Prosecutor Sandra

____ 20. HEART   T. Sal got information about the robbery from him.

____ 21. OSVALDO   U. Mr. Harmon dreamed Steve would go to ____ and play football.

____ 22. TONY   V. Witness who saw King and Bobo in the store

____ 23. TESTIFY   W. Ma'am, it's just routine. Don't ____ about it.

____ 24. BOLDEN   X. He was beaten up in the park.

____ 25. MORAL   Y. They were not allowed in the visitor's area.

Monster Multiple Choice Unit Test 2 Page 2

II. Matching

1. Which of these is NOT one of Osvaldo's actions that O'Brien points out to show he is not a fearful person?
    A. He fought a member of the Diablos gang.
    B. He cut a stranger in the face.
    C. He beat up his girlfriend.
    D. He beat up Tony in the park.

2. What is the guard's reaction to Steve's gagging when cleaning the floors?
    A. He said, "You vomit–you just got more to clean up!"
    B. He started gagging, too, and vomited on the floor.
    C. He laughed at Steve.
    D. He said, "What a pansy! Not even man enough to clean a floor without gagging!"

3. Describe Steve's reaction to Dr. Moody's testimony about how Mr. Nesbitt actually died. What was James King's reaction to it?
    A. Steve starts to cry. King catches his breath sharply.
    B. Steve catches his breath sharply. King listens to it without any sign of caring.
    C. Steve cringes. King laughs.
    D. Steve looks solemn. King smirks.

4. According to Bobo, was the shooting of Mr. Nesbitt accidental?
    A. No, it wasn't. King said he "had to light him up because he was trying to muscle him."
    B. Yes, Nesbitt fired his gun as King was bumping into him; Nesbitt actually shot himself.
    C. Yes, he said the gun "just went off" when King and Nesbitt were wrestling.
    D. No, it wasn't. Bobo testified that Nesbitt drew first, and King shot him in self-defense.

5. Steve says, "Maybe we are here _____."
    A. to show our humanity
    B. as actors in the film of life
    C. because we lie to ourselves
    D. simply because someone has to be

6. Why does O'Brien decide Steve should testify?
    A. The others testifying are making him look bad.
    B. She wants to put as much distance between Steve and King as possible, and to present Steve as someone the jurors can believe in.
    C. O'Brien wants the jury to see Steve is sorry for participating in the robbery/murder.
    D. She wants to hear the truth, under oath, directly from Steve.

Monster Multiple Choice Unit Test 2 Page 3

7. Does Steve tell the truth on the witness stand?
   A. No
   B. Yes
   C. It depends on the jury.
   D. He thought he did.

8. What main point is NOT a part of Briggs's closing arguments to the jury?
   A. Bobo implicates King because the police have him on a criminal matter and have offered him a deal if he comes here and implicates someone else.
   B. Mrs. Henry's mind was on her granddaughter; she could have been mistaken about King's identity.
   C. King was desperate to acquire some money; he was broke.
   D. This case is about whether or not you believe people who are admitted participants in this crime and who are saving their own hides. If you believe that their positions, their stated characters, so taint their testimony that everything they say is well within the area of reasonable doubt, then you have no choice but to find Mr. King not guilty.

9. What main point is NOT one O'Brien makes in her final arguments to the jury?
   A. The State did not even suggest that Mr. Harmon was in the store at the time of the robbery.
   B. Mr. Harmon was not with Bobo and King eating chicken after the crime.
   C. Mr. Harmon answered questions openly and honestly on the stand and is of a much better character than the others who took the stand.
   D. Steve has no prior criminal record.

10. What is O'Brien's reaction to Steve's open arms to give her a hug?
   A. At first she reaches to hug him back, but then turns away.
   B. She gives him a brief and professional hug then turns away.
   C. O'Brien says, "Goodbye. Good luck." And she walks past him.
   D. She stiffens and turns to pick up papers on the table.

11. What is the last image of Steve in the film?
   A. He turns towards the camera with outstretched arms. The picture turns grainy/distorted. He looks like a monster.
   B. He is holding his camera, filming an image of himself in a mirror.
   C. He is home with his family, playing Batman and Robin with Jerry.
   D. He is alone on the courthouse steps.

12. What final question is Steve trying to answer?
   A. Why did I agree to go check out the store?
   B. What did Miss O'Brien see that caused her to turn away from me?
   C. What will I do with my life now?
   D. What is truth?

Monster Multiple Choice Unit Test 2 Page 4

III. Quotations

Match the speaker to the quote.

    A. Steve Harmon   B. Petrocelli   C. O'Brien   D. Mr. Sawicki

    E. Bolden   F. Briggs   G. Bobo   H. King

1. I know what right is, what truth is. I don't do tightropes, moral or otherwise.

2. I didn't say a magic word and turn into somebody different. But here I am, maybe on the verge of losing my life, or the life I used to have.

3. Then, we got some fried chicken and some wedgies and some sodas.

4. You should have said, "I didn't do it."

5. But there are monsters in our communities–people who are willing to steal and to kill, people who disregard the rights of others.

6. I just wanted to do the right thing. You know, like a good citizen.

7. When you make a film, you leave an impression on the viewers, who serve as a kind of jury for your film.

8. What did she see?

Monster Multiple Choice Unit Test 2 Page 5

IV. Vocabulary

____ 1. PROCEEDS   A. Event

____ 2. GRUESOME   B. Upheld; supported; maintained

____ 3. PAN   C. Bizarre; distorted; incongruous

____ 4. CACOPHONY   D. Bring forth

____ 5. UNSHACKLE   E. Causes an adverse judgement to be made before facts are considered

____ 6. MOSAIC   F. Keep from

____ 7. CORRIDOR   G. Trusted advisor or counselor

____ 8. MENTOR   H. Take off chains or restraints

____ 9. PREMISES   I. Implies involvement

____10. CONCENTRIC   J. Complete loss of courage in the face of trouble

____11. PRECIOUS   K. Permanently handing over to

____12. IMPLICATES   L. Horrifying; shocking

____13. PREJUDICES   M. Slow, systematic camera movement to show a large view

____14. TRAUMA   N. People guilty of a crime

____15. CONSIGNING   O. Having a common center

____16. GROTESQUE   P. Money obtained from a venture

____17. MERELY   Q. Ruined through clumsiness

____18. VICIOUSLY   R. Picture or design made up of small pieces

____19. DEPRIVE   S. Valuable

____20. ELICIT   T. Only; simply

____21. BOTCHED   U. Jumbled, discordant sounds

____22. DISMAY   V. Hallway

____23. SUSTAINED   W. Land and/or buildings

____24. CULPRITS   X. Wound produced from sudden injury

____25. INCIDENT   Y. Violently with mean or evil intent

V. Essay

     Steve said, "I wanted to open my shirt and tell her to look into my heart to see who I really was, who the real Steve Harmon was." Who is the real Steve Harmon? What would she see if she looked into his heart? Use information from the text to support your answer.

MULTIPLE CHOICE UNIT TEST ANSWER SHEET
Monster

	Match	Multiple Choice	Quotes	Vocab
1				
2				
3				
4				
5				
6				
7				
8				
9			■	
10			■	
11			■	
12			■	
13		■	■	
14		■	■	
15		■	■	
16		■	■	
17		■	■	
18		■	■	
19		■	■	
20		■	■	
21		■	■	
22		■	■	
23		■	■	
24		■	■	
25		■	■	

MULTIPLE CHOICE UNIT TEST 1 ANSWER KEY
Monster

	Match	Multiple Choice	Quotes	Vocab
1	I	A	B	U
2	K	D	F	L
3	T	C	C	O
4	W	D	G	D
5	P	C	H	I
6	V	B	D	G
7	N	B	A	Q
8	Y	D	E	M
9	G	A		V
10	F	C		K
11	M	C		J
12	C	B		S
13	J			W
14	L			Y
15	X			R
16	U			E
17	H			F
18	R			C
19	Q			H
20	A			X
21	S			T
22	E			N
23	D			B
24	O			A
25	B			P

MULTIPLE CHOICE UNIT TEST 2 ANSWER KEY
Monster

	Match	Multiple Choice	Quotes	Vocab
1	E	D	A	P
2	Y	A	A	L
3	A	B	G	M
4	S	A	C	U
5	F	C	B	H
6	R	B	G	R
7	W	A	D	V
8	D	C	A	G
9	Q	D		W
10	O	D		O
11	P	A		S
12	L	B		I
13	I			E
14	H			X
15	B			K
16	N			C
17	V			T
18	U			Y
19	J			F
20	M			D
21	G			Q
22	X			J
23	C			B
24	T			N
25	K			A

UNIT RESOURCE MATERIALS

EXTRA ACTIVITIES

One of the difficulties in teaching a novel is that all students don't read at the same speed. One student who likes to read may take the book home and finish it in a day or two. Sometimes a few students finish the in-class assignments early. The problem, then, is finding suitable extra activities for students.

One thing that helps is to keep a little library in the classroom. For this unit on *Monster*, you might check out from the school library other related books and articles about cold case files, psychology, the criminal justice system, films and film-making, neighborhood watch programs, hotlines for help, community programs for youth, or social services. Some students might like to read other books by Walter Dean Myers.

The other things you may keep on hand are word search or crossword puzzles. We have made some of them relating directly to *Monster* for you. Feel free to duplicate them for your class.

Some students may like to draw. You might devise a contest or allow some extra-credit grade for students who draw characters or scenes from *Monster*. Note, too, that if the students do not want to keep their drawings you may pick up some extra bulletin board materials this way. If you have a contest and you supply the prize, you could, possibly, make the drawing itself a non-refundable entry fee.

MORE ACTIVITIES *Monster*

1. Have students design a book cover (front and back and inside flaps) for *Monster*.

2. Have students design a bulletin board (ready to be put up; not just sketched) for *Monster*.

3. Take a class field trip to the courthouse to see what actually goes on there.

4. Use some of the related topics (noted earlier for an in-class library) as topics for research, reports or written papers, or as topics for guest speakers.

5. Actually act out the book (with minimal scenery, props, and costumes) and perform it for another English class or two.

6. A newspaper unit could parallel this unit or immediately follow it. Students could use the facts of the book *Monster* to write a news story, an editorial, an obituary, a comic strip, an advertisement, etc. You could study the parts of the newspaper, and compare and contrast the newspaper with on-line news or the newspaper's on-line site. Use the various kinds of writing in the newspaper to further explore point of view: the obituary, for example, would be written from a different point of view than an editorial.

7. Further explore the idea of "Who am I?" with your students. Steve takes pictures of himself from all different angles, in different clothes, etc. to get "one true picture" of himself. Encourage your students to create one true picture of themselves, a self-portrait either in writing or perhaps through drawing, film, a collage, or however they can.

8. Have students interview each other, as if they are detectives, to find out the answer to the question, "Who am I?" regarding the person they interview. After the interviews, students should each write a short composition describing the person they interviewed. The "interview-ees" might find it enlightening or interesting, at least, to read the compositions written about themselves. Providing students with a list of questions to ask (or brainstorming this list as a class) would probably help the interviews be more meaningful.

9. Another exercise in exploring point of view would be to have students all attend the same event–say a school sports event or dance–and then have them each write a composition describing the event. Each person would see the event from a slightly different point of view.

BULLETIN BOARD IDEAS
Monster

1. Save one corner of the board for the best of students' writing assignments.

2. Take one of the word search puzzles from the extra activities packet and (with a marker) copy it over in a large size on the bulletin board. Write the clue words to one side. Invite students prior to and after class to find the words and circle them on the bulletin board.

3. Create a bulletin board about each of the careers your students researched. Post their fact sheets with a picture of someone showing the career.

4. Create a "Movie" bulletin board for *Monster*. Make big film frames and fill each with quotes or pictures representing different aspects or characters from the book.

5. Make a "Who am I?" bulletin board. Place a mirror–or highly reflective surface of some sort (maybe tinfoil?) in the center. All around it place your students' pictures in cut-out "frames." Write in the words: student, daughter, son, athlete, musician, artist, scientist, friend, nephew, etc. to show all the roles of the students in your classroom. Maybe brainstorm these words together as a class and write them up as students suggest them.

6. Take pictures of your school from all different points of view: looking out from the principal's office, from the gymnasium, from a bus driver's seat, from the stands by your football field, from the stage, from the cafeteria, from the science lab, the custodian's closet, etc. Post the pictures in "frames" on the board. Get students to tell you where each picture is taken from, label the picture, and talk about what "school" is from that person's perspective.

7. Do an oral, class writing project. Pretend the jury came back with a "guilty" verdict for Steven. Have students write a new ending for the book. How would the ending of the book been different if Steve had been found guilty? Would the ending have been written in his notebook? What would the camera see? How would the meaning of the book change, and to what would it change? Use the bulletin board to write the final version of the story. Title the board: GUILTY. Maybe write the story up on the bulletin board and then draw thick bars like a jail cell over it.

Monster Word List

No.	Word	Clue/Definition
1.	BATMAN	Jerry wanted Steve to be this superhero.
2.	BELT	They take away your shoelaces and this in jail so you can't kill yourself.
3.	BIBLE	Mama brought this book to Steve.
4.	BOBO	Richard Evans
5.	BOLDEN	Sal got information about the robbery from him.
6.	COLLEGE	Mr. Harmon dreamed Steve would go to ___ and play football.
7.	DIABLOS	Gang Osvaldo joined
8.	DO	What did I __? What did I __?
9.	ERNIE	He didn't think he was guilty because he didn't take anything out of the store.
10.	GUILTY	Jury's verdict for King
11.	GUN	The murder weapon
12.	HARMON	Steve's last name
13.	HEART	I wanted to open my shirt and tell her to look into my ___ to see who I really was.
14.	HENRY	Witness who saw King and Bobo in the store
15.	HUG	Steve tries to give one to O'Brien
16.	HUMAN	O'Brien said part of her job was to make Steve look ___ in the eyes of the jury.
17.	JAIL	Steve's parents visited him there.
18.	JERRY	Steve's younger brother
19.	JOSE	He found the body.
20.	JURY	Twelve people who decide the verdict
21.	KARYL	Detective who wanted the death penalty
22.	KIDS	They were not allowed in the visitor's area.
23.	KING	He was on trial with Steve.
24.	LIE	Maybe we are here because we ___ to ourselves.
25.	LOOKOUT	Steve's job in the robbery
26.	MONEY	Steve did not get any of it from the robbery.
27.	MONSTER	Steve looks like one at the end of the film.
28.	MOORE	She testified that King was at her house.
29.	MORAL	Petrocelli said Steve made a ___ decision to participate in the robbery
30.	MYERS	Author Walter Dean
31.	NESBITT	He was killed.
32.	NOTEBOOK	Steve wrote his script and notes in it.
33.	OBRIEN	Defense attorney Kathy
34.	OSVALDO	He was to detain anyone chasing the robbers.
35.	PAID	Phrase King used regarding the robbery: getting ___
36.	PETROCELLI	Prosecutor Sandra
37.	PICTURES	O'Brien wanted to see Steve's reaction to these she put on the table.
38.	SAWICKI	Film club sponsor; character witness for Steve
39.	SMILE	I felt embarrassed that a ___ would mean so much.
40.	SOUL	All they can do is put me in jail. They can't touch my ___.
41.	STEVE	Narrator on trial for murder
42.	TESTIFY	Witnesses do this in court.
43.	TOMORROWS	Think about all the ___ of your life.
44.	TONY	He was beaten up in the park.
45.	TRUTH	Steve said truth is this.
46.	WORRY	Ma'am, it's just routine. Don't ___ about it.
47.	ZINZI	He called Detective Gluck.

WORD SEARCH Monster

```
C T O M O R R O W S Z Q V T M X Q J T V V
R W X P Z X W Z W B W V C P N P B T X J S
M K X T R B V W C G D M T Z E N Y F Q M Y
R L K Y M X K D Y M V B X T T L J K C F B
K F D R Z L S H D H J N R D R Z K H N V J
W X N D W N A T I M L O P C Q B H Y B P R
F Y L P Y S W Q A H C X M H J R T K A X M
P B B C H V I H B E T J T S D L N Y T Z F
A O P K G H C G L A S H E O A S O H M V M
I B E A E U K L O R E T F R N B M H A O M
D O C R J A I L S T R W O R R Y Z I N Z I
Z R O Y N E N L X U U M Q I R Y Z S L F R
T O L L K I G Y T K T V E U V L T M T E Z
M D L F H J E H C Y C N J N P E T R H J S
B H E K T R O Q F J I W N N R H E N R Y N
E S G D I D M K X O P O V L Z A S M N T C
L R E W L D D G X S T L N C W R T O S J X
T S T A S F S L P E P F O L M M I N D V Z
D R V N E D L O B S O U L O C O F E H G X
P S N A V M M O Y I B S J P K N Y Y Y U N
O U B M E G O H N F B G Z G V O P V G K G
G X Y U T K M Y E R S L H J L K U L C J W
R S X H S N E S B I T T E S P N K T G K R
```

BATMAN	GUN	KARYL	NESBITT	STEVE
BELT	HARMON	KIDS	NOTEBOOK	TESTIFY
BIBLE	HEART	KING	OBRIEN	TOMORROWS
BOBO	HENRY	LIE	OSVALDO	TONY
BOLDEN	HUG	LOOKOUT	PAID	TRUTH
COLLEGE	HUMAN	MONEY	PETROCELLI	WORRY
DIABLOS	JAIL	MONSTER	PICTURES	ZINZI
DO	JERRY	MOORE	SAWICKI	
ERNIE	JOSE	MORAL	SMILE	
GUILTY	JURY	MYERS	SOUL	

WORD SEARCH ANSWER KEY Monster

BATMAN	GUN	KARYL	NESBITT	STEVE
BELT	HARMON	KIDS	NOTEBOOK	TESTIFY
BIBLE	HEART	KING	OBRIEN	TOMORROWS
BOBO	HENRY	LIE	OSVALDO	TONY
BOLDEN	HUG	LOOKOUT	PAID	TRUTH
COLLEGE	HUMAN	MONEY	PETROCELLI	WORRY
DIABLOS	JAIL	MONSTER	PICTURES	ZINZI
DO	JERRY	MOORE	SAWICKI	
ERNIE	JOSE	MORAL	SMILE	
GUILTY	JURY	MYERS	SOUL	

CROSSWORD Monster

Across
1. What did I __? What did I __?
3. Author Walter Dean
7. Richard Evans
8. He was beaten up in the park.
10. Maybe we are here because we ___ to ourselves.
11. Steve's parents visited him there.
13. They were not allowed in the visitor's area.
14. They take away your shoelaces and this in jail so you can't kill yourself.
15. Steve's last name
18. The murder weapon
19. Steve's younger brother
21. Detective who wanted the death penalty
22. Witnesses do this in court.
24. I wanted to open my shirt and tell her to look into my ___ to see who I really was.
25. Mr. Harmon dreamed Steve would go to ___ and play football.
26. Mama brought this book to Steve.

Down
2. Defense attorney Kathy
3. Steve looks like one at the end of the film.
4. He didn't think he was guilty because he didn't take anything out of the store.
5. Narrator on trial for murder
6. He called Detective Gluck.
9. Steve wrote his script and notes in it.
11. He found the body.
12. Sal got information about the robbery from him.
13. He was on trial with Steve.
15. Witness who saw King and Bobo in the store
16. Steve did not get any of it from the robbery.
17. He was killed.
19. Twelve people who decide the verdict
20. I felt embarrassed that a ___ would mean so much.
23. All they can do is put me in jail. They can't touch my ___.
24. Steve tries to give one to O'Brien

CROSSWORD ANSWER KEY Monster

			1 D	2 O			3 M	Y	4 E	R	5 S		
		6 Z		7 B	O	B	O		R		8 T	O	9 N	Y
10 L	I	E		R			N		N		E		O	
		N		11 J	A	I	L		S	I	V	T	12 B
		Z		O		E		T		E	E	E	O
13 K	I	D	S		N		E				14 B	E	L	T
I					15 E		16 H	A	R	17 M	O	N		O	D
N					E			O		E		O		E
18 G	U	N			N			N		S		K		N
			19 J	E	R	R	Y		E	B		20 S
			U		Y			Y		I		M
	21 K	A	R	Y	L			22 T	E	23 S	T	I	F	Y
			Y		24 H	E	A	R	T	O		L
					U					U		E
	25 C	O	L	L	E	G	E		26 B	I	B	L	E

Across
1. What did I __? What did I __?
3. Author Walter Dean
7. Richard Evans
8. He was beaten up in the park.
10. Maybe we are here because we ___ to ourselves.
11. Steve's parents visited him there.
13. They were not allowed in the visitor's area.
14. They take away your shoelaces and this in jail so you can't kill yourself.
15. Steve's last name
18. The murder weapon
19. Steve's younger brother
21. Detective who wanted the death penalty
22. Witnesses do this in court.
24. I wanted to open my shirt and tell her to look into my ___ to see who I really was.
25. Mr. Harmon dreamed Steve would go to ___ and play football.
26. Mama brought this book to Steve.

Down
2. Defense attorney Kathy
3. Steve looks like one at the end of the film.
4. He didn't think he was guilty because he didn't take anything out of the store.
5. Narrator on trial for murder
6. He called Detective Gluck.
9. Steve wrote his script and notes in it.
11. He found the body.
12. Sal got information about the robbery from him.
13. He was on trial with Steve.
15. Witness who saw King and Bobo in the store
16. Steve did not get any of it from the robbery.
17. He was killed.
19. Twelve people who decide the verdict
20. I felt embarrassed that a ___ would mean so much.
23. All they can do is put me in jail. They can't touch my ___.
24. Steve tries to give one to O'Brien

MATCHING 1 Monster

___ 1. SAWICKI   A. Steve tries to give one to O'Brien

___ 2. HEART   B. Sal got information about the robbery from him.

___ 3. HENRY   C. He called Detective Gluck.

___ 4. ERNIE   D. Richard Evans

___ 5. OBRIEN   E. Witness who saw King and Bobo in the store

___ 6. WORRY   F. He was to detain anyone chasing the robbers.

___ 7. NOTEBOOK   G. Author Walter Dean

___ 8. BOLDEN   H. Steve's younger brother

___ 9. MONEY   I. Film club sponsor; character witness for Steve

___ 10. JOSE   J. Steve wrote his script and notes in it.

___ 11. BOBO   K. He was beaten up in the park.

___ 12. STEVE   L. All they can do is put me in jail. They can't touch my ___.

___ 13. OSVALDO   M. He found the body.

___ 14. HARMON   N. O'Brien said part of her job was to make Steve look ___ in the eyes of the jury.

___ 15. LIE   O. I wanted to open my shirt and tell her to look into my ___ to see who I really was.

___ 16. MYERS   P. Narrator on trial for murder

___ 17. HUMAN   Q. Defense attorney Kathy

___ 18. BIBLE   R. Steve did not get any of it from the robbery.

___ 19. PAID   S. Maybe we are here because we ___ to ourselves.

___ 20. TONY   T. Mama brought this book to Steve.

___ 21. ZINZI   U. He didn't think he was guilty because he didn't take anything out of the store.

___ 22. LOOKOUT   V. Phrase King used regarding the robbery: getting ___

___ 23. JERRY   W. Steve's last name

___ 24. SOUL   X. Steve's job in the robbery

___ 25. HUG   Y. Ma'am, it's just routine. Don't ___ about it.

MATCHING 1 ANSWER KEY Monster

I - 1.	SAWICKI	A. Steve tries to give one to O'Brien
O - 2.	HEART	B. Sal got information about the robbery from him.
E - 3.	HENRY	C. He called Detective Gluck.
U - 4.	ERNIE	D. Richard Evans
Q - 5.	OBRIEN	E. Witness who saw King and Bobo in the store
Y - 6.	WORRY	F. He was to detain anyone chasing the robbers.
J - 7.	NOTEBOOK	G. Author Walter Dean
B - 8.	BOLDEN	H. Steve's younger brother
R - 9.	MONEY	I. Film club sponsor; character witness for Steve
M - 10.	JOSE	J. Steve wrote his script and notes in it.
D - 11.	BOBO	K. He was beaten up in the park.
P - 12.	STEVE	L. All they can do is put me in jail. They can't touch my ___.
F - 13.	OSVALDO	M. He found the body.
W - 14.	HARMON	N. O'Brien said part of her job was to make Steve look ___ in the eyes of the jury.
S - 15.	LIE	O. I wanted to open my shirt and tell her to look into my ___ to see who I really was.
G - 16.	MYERS	P. Narrator on trial for murder
N - 17.	HUMAN	Q. Defense attorney Kathy
T - 18.	BIBLE	R. Steve did not get any of it from the robbery.
V - 19.	PAID	S. Maybe we are here because we ___ to ourselves.
K - 20.	TONY	T. Mama brought this book to Steve.
C - 21.	ZINZI	U. He didn't think he was guilty because he didn't take anything out of the store.
X - 22.	LOOKOUT	V. Phrase King used regarding the robbery: getting ___
H - 23.	JERRY	W. Steve's last name
L - 24.	SOUL	X. Steve's job in the robbery
A - 25.	HUG	Y. Ma'am, it's just routine. Don't ___ about it.

MATCHING 2 Monster

___ 1. KING A. Detective who wanted the death penalty
___ 2. HUG B. Steve looks like one at the end of the film.
___ 3. MONSTER C. He was on trial with Steve.
___ 4. HUMAN D. Phrase King used regarding the robbery: getting ___
___ 5. OSVALDO E. Sal got information about the robbery from him.
___ 6. BATMAN F. Maybe we are here because we ___ to ourselves.
___ 7. NOTEBOOK G. Richard Evans
___ 8. ZINZI H. I felt embarrassed that a ___ would mean so much.
___ 9. BIBLE I. Steve's younger brother
___ 10. HENRY J. He called Detective Gluck.
___ 11. BOBO K. All they can do is put me in jail. They can't touch my ___.
___ 12. MYERS L. O'Brien said part of her job was to make Steve look ___ in the eyes of the jury.
___ 13. KARYL M. He was to detain anyone chasing the robbers.
___ 14. SAWICKI N. Author Walter Dean
___ 15. LIE O. Film club sponsor; character witness for Steve
___ 16. BOLDEN P. I wanted to open my shirt and tell her to look into my ___ to see who I really was.
___ 17. OBRIEN Q. Witness who saw King and Bobo in the store
___ 18. SOUL R. Steve tries to give one to O'Brien
___ 19. SMILE S. Defense attorney Kathy
___ 20. JERRY T. Steve wrote his script and notes in it.
___ 21. JOSE U. He found the body.
___ 22. HEART V. They take away your shoelaces and this in jail so you can't kill yourself.
___ 23. PAID W. Jerry wanted Steve to be this superhero.
___ 24. TESTIFY X. Mama brought this book to Steve.
___ 25. BELT Y. Witnesses do this in court.

MATCHING 2 ANSWER KEY Monster

C - 1. KING	A.	Detective who wanted the death penalty
R - 2. HUG	B.	Steve looks like one at the end of the film.
B - 3. MONSTER	C.	He was on trial with Steve.
L - 4. HUMAN	D.	Phrase King used regarding the robbery: getting ___
M - 5. OSVALDO	E.	Sal got information about the robbery from him.
W - 6. BATMAN	F.	Maybe we are here because we ___ to ourselves.
T - 7. NOTEBOOK	G.	Richard Evans
J - 8. ZINZI	H.	I felt embarrassed that a ___ would mean so much.
X - 9. BIBLE	I.	Steve's younger brother
Q -10. HENRY	J.	He called Detective Gluck.
G -11. BOBO	K.	All they can do is put me in jail. They can't touch my ___.
N -12. MYERS	L.	O'Brien said part of her job was to make Steve look ___ in the eyes of the jury.
A -13. KARYL	M.	He was to detain anyone chasing the robbers.
O -14. SAWICKI	N.	Author Walter Dean
F -15. LIE	O.	Film club sponsor; character witness for Steve
E -16. BOLDEN	P.	I wanted to open my shirt and tell her to look into my ___ to see who I really was.
S -17. OBRIEN	Q.	Witness who saw King and Bobo in the store
K -18. SOUL	R.	Steve tries to give one to O'Brien
H -19. SMILE	S.	Defense attorney Kathy
I - 20. JERRY	T.	Steve wrote his script and notes in it.
U -21. JOSE	U.	He found the body.
P -22. HEART	V.	They take away your shoelaces and this in jail so you can't kill yourself.
D -23. PAID	W.	Jerry wanted Steve to be this superhero.
Y -24. TESTIFY	X.	Mama brought this book to Steve.
V -25. BELT	Y.	Witnesses do this in court.

JUGGLE LETTERS Monster

1. LONBDE = 1. _____
   Sal got information about the robbery from him.

2. AWKISIC = 2. _____
   Film club sponsor; character witness for Steve

3. BROENI = 3. _____
   Defense attorney Kathy

4. TLUGYI = 4. _____
   Jury's verdict for King

5. YALRK = 5. _____
   Detective who wanted the death penalty

6. IAJL = 6. _____
   Steve's parents visited him there.

7. OBOB = 7. _____
   Richard Evans

8. BLET = 8. _____
   They take away your shoelaces and this in jail so you can't kill yourself.

9. DISK = 9. _____
   They were not allowed in the visitor's area.

10. UMNHA =10. _____
    O'Brien said part of her job was to make Steve look ___ in the eyes of the jury.

11. LSUO =11. _____
    All they can do is put me in jail. They can't touch my ___.

12. RENYH =12. _____
    Witness who saw King and Bobo in the store

13. NMYEO =13. _____
    Steve did not get any of it from the robbery.

14. NIZIZ =14. _____
    He called Detective Gluck.

15. LEEOGCL =15. _____
    Mr. Harmon dreamed Steve would go to ___ and play football.

16. NMSRTEO =16. _____
Steve looks like one at the end of the film.

17. KOUTOOL =17. _____
Steve's job in the robbery

18. AOVSDOL =18. _____
He was to detain anyone chasing the robbers.

19. GUN =19. _____
The murder weapon

20. NTYO =20. _____
He was beaten up in the park.

21. BNOKEOTO =21. _____
Steve wrote his script and notes in it.

22. SOTWRORMO =22. _____
Think about all the ___ of your life.

23. YORWR =23. _____
Ma'am, it's just routine. Don't ___ about it.

24. DAPI =24. _____
Phrase King used regarding the robbery: getting ___

25. ETVSE =25. _____
Narrator on trial for murder

26. SEOJ =26. _____
He found the body.

27. NKGI =27. _____
He was on trial with Steve.

28. ITENSTB =28. _____
He was killed.

29. ROEMO =29. _____
She testified that King was at her house.

30. GUH =30. _____
Steve tries to give one to O'Brien

31. RESMY =31. _____
Author Walter Dean

32. LBIOADS =32. _____
Gang Osvaldo joined

148

33. LILOCPETRE   =33. _____
                  Prosecutor Sandra

34. MANATB   =34. _____
                  Jerry wanted Steve to be this superhero.

35. LBBIE   =35. _____
                  Mama brought this book to Steve.

36. YRJU   =36. _____
                  Twelve people who decide the verdict

37. ILE   =37. _____
                  Maybe we are here because we ___ to ourselves.

38. RMNHOA   =38. _____
                  Steve's last name

39. RTHUT   =39. _____
                  Steve said truth is this.

40. EMSIL   =40. _____
                  I felt embarrassed that a ___ would mean so much.

41. IRUETSPC   =41. _____
                  O'Brien wanted to see Steve's reaction to these she put on the table.

42. FITTYES   =42. _____
                  Witnesses do this in court.

43. NREEI   =43. _____
                  He didn't think he was guilty because he didn't take anything out of the store.

44. AMLOR   =44. _____
                  Petrocelli said Steve made a ___ decision to participate in the robbery

45. OD   =45. _____
                  What did I __? What did I __?

46. ATEHR   =46. _____
                  I wanted to open my shirt and tell her to look into my ___ to see who I really was.

47. ERJYR   =47. _____
                  Steve's younger brother

JUGGLE LETTERS ANSWER KEY Monster

1. LONBDE = 1. BOLDEN
   Sal got information about the robbery from him.

2. AWKISIC = 2. SAWICKI
   Film club sponsor; character witness for Steve

3. BROENI = 3. OBRIEN
   Defense attorney Kathy

4. TLUGYI = 4. GUILTY
   Jury's verdict for King

5. YALRK = 5. KARYL
   Detective who wanted the death penalty

6. IAJL = 6. JAIL
   Steve's parents visited him there.

7. OBOB = 7. BOBO
   Richard Evans

8. BLET = 8. BELT
   They take away your shoelaces and this in jail so you can't kill yourself.

9. DISK = 9. KIDS
   They were not allowed in the visitor's area.

10. UMNHA =10. HUMAN
    O'Brien said part of her job was to make Steve look ___ in the eyes of the jury.

11. LSUO =11. SOUL
    All they can do is put me in jail. They can't touch my ___.

12. RENYH =12. HENRY
    Witness who saw King and Bobo in the store

13. NMYEO =13. MONEY
    Steve did not get any of it from the robbery.

14. NIZIZ =14. ZINZI
    He called Detective Gluck.

15. LEEOGCL =15. COLLEGE
    Mr. Harmon dreamed Steve would go to ___ and play football.

16. NMSRTEO =16. MONSTER
Steve looks like one at the end of the film.

17. KOUTOOL =17. LOOKOUT
Steve's job in the robbery

18. AOVSDOL =18. OSVALDO
He was to detain anyone chasing the robbers.

19. GUN =19. GUN
The murder weapon

20. NTYO =20. TONY
He was beaten up in the park.

21. BNOKEOTO =21. NOTEBOOK
Steve wrote his script and notes in it.

22. SOTWRORMO =22. TOMORROWS
Think about all the ___ of your life.

23. YORWR =23. WORRY
Ma'am, it's just routine. Don't ___ about it.

24. DAPI =24. PAID
Phrase King used regarding the robbery: getting ___

25. ETVSE =25. STEVE
Narrator on trial for murder

26. SEOJ =26. JOSE
He found the body.

27. NKGI =27. KING
He was on trial with Steve.

28. ITENSTB =28. NESBITT
He was killed.

29. ROEMO =29. MOORE
She testified that King was at her house.

30. GUH =30. HUG
Steve tries to give one to O'Brien

31. RESMY =31. MYERS
Author Walter Dean

32. LBIOADS =32. DIABLOS
Gang Osvaldo joined

33. LILOCPETRE =33. PETROCELLI
Prosecutor Sandra

34. MANATB =34. BATMAN
Jerry wanted Steve to be this superhero.

35. LBBIE =35. BIBLE
Mama brought this book to Steve.

36. YRJU =36. JURY
Twelve people who decide the verdict

37. ILE =37. LIE
Maybe we are here because we ___ to ourselves.

38. RMNHOA =38. HARMON
Steve's last name

39. RTHUT =39. TRUTH
Steve said truth is this.

40. EMSIL =40. SMILE
I felt embarrassed that a ___ would mean so much.

41. IRUETSPC =41. PICTURES
O'Brien wanted to see Steve's reaction to these she put on the table.

42. FITTYES =42. TESTIFY
Witnesses do this in court.

43. NREEI =43. ERNIE
He didn't think he was guilty because he didn't take anything out of the store.

44. AMLOR =44. MORAL
Petrocelli said Steve made a ___ decision to participate in the robbery

45. OD =45. DO
What did I __? What did I __?

46. ATEHR =46. HEART
I wanted to open my shirt and tell her to look into my ___ to see who I really was.

47. ERJYR =47. JERRY
Steve's younger brother

VOCABULARY RESOURCE MATERIALS

Monster Vocabulary Word List

No.	Word	Clue/Definition
1.	ACCOMPLICE	Helper in an illegal act
2.	ACCUSATIONS	Charges of wrongdoings
3.	ACQUAINTANCE	Person one knows casually
4.	ADJOURN	Suspend proceedings until another time
5.	ADMISSIBLE	Can be allowed in
6.	APPREHENDED	Caught
7.	ASHY	Pale; light-colored
8.	BOTCHED	Ruined through clumsiness
9.	CACOPHONY	Jumbled, discordant sounds
10.	COMPASSION	Feeling or sharing the suffering of another in the intent of giving aid, support, or showing mercy
11.	CONCENTRIC	Having a common center
12.	CONDESCENDINGLY	With an air of superiority
13.	CONSIGNING	Permanently handing over to
14.	CONSPIRATORS	People who plan an illegal or evil act
15.	CONTENTION	Point put forth in an argument
16.	CORRIDOR	Hallway
17.	COUNSEL	Attorney; one who gives advise
18.	CULPRITS	People guilty of a crime
19.	DEPRIVE	Keep from
20.	DISMAY	Complete loss of courage in the face of trouble
21.	DISTINGUISH	Recognize apart from others
22.	ELICIT	Bring forth
23.	EMPHATICALLY	Boldly; definitely; accented
24.	EVIDENT	Clear; obvious; easily seen
25.	GRACE	Mercy or good will of God
26.	GROTESQUE	Bizarre; distorted; incongruous
27.	GRUESOME	Horrifying; shocking
28.	GULLIBLE	Easily deceived
29.	HESITATION	Holding back for reason of uncertainty
30.	IMPEDE	Block; get in the way of
31.	IMPLICATES	Implies involvement
32.	INCIDENT	Event
33.	INFER	Conclude from evidence
34.	MENTOR	Trusted advisor or counselor
35.	MERELY	Only; simply
36.	METHODICALLY	Proceeding in a systematic order
37.	MORAL	Arising from the sense of right and wrong
38.	MOSAIC	Picture or design made up of small pieces
39.	OBSCENE	Vulgar; offensive; indecent
40.	PAN	Slow, systematic camera movement to show a large view
41.	PAROLE	The release of a prisoner before his term has expired
42.	PERPETRATOR	One who commits a crime
43.	PODIUM	Elevated platform for a speaker or conductor
44.	PRECIOUS	Valuable
45.	PRECISE	Clearly expressed; distinct and correct in sound or statement
46.	PREJUDICES	Causes an adverse judgement to be made before facts are considered
47.	PREMISES	Land and/or buildings
48.	PRESUMABLY	Reasonably assumed
49.	PROCEEDS	Money obtained from a venture

Monster Vocabulary Word List Continued

50.	PURSUER	One who chases after
51.	SALVATION	Deliverance from evil or difficulty
52.	SILHOUETTED	Outlined or showing dark against light
53.	SOLE	Single
54.	SUICIDE	Intentionally killing oneself
55.	SUSTAINED	Upheld; supported; maintained
56.	TRANSCRIBED	Written down
57.	TRAUMA	Wound produced from sudden injury
58.	UNSHACKLE	Take off chains or restraints
59.	VERDICT	Decision from a jury
60.	VERIFY	Prove the truth of
61.	VICIOUSLY	Violently with mean or evil intent

VOCABULARY WORD SEARCH Monster

```
P G L C O N S I G N I N G C P A M P C V A
Y R S X S B H M L Q F O I A A D L E O I C
P O E J Z Q S G G S P I N C R M C R N C Q
Y T T J C X G C W Q F T C O O I Y P T I U
L E S N U O C E E Z V A I P L S K E E O A
G S U B B D Q L L N P V D H E S Q T N U I
N Q O T R Z I K B V E L E O M I E R T S N
W U I L O M P C D Y A A N N Q B C A I L T
Z E C Y D G R A E L C S T Y F L I T O Y A
P D E G I U E H B S C Z W D Z E L O N X N
P Q R K R L C S N D U V L E T A P R X D C
D R P L R L I N B E S M V N P M M H P E E
I N O E O I S U R P A S E I G U O D R H D
S R F C C B E N N R T D Q A G A C R E C E
T N F A E L M P D I I M X T R R C Y M T D
I E M O S E U R G V O H E S I T A T I O N
N D D R N H D L E E N C T U U M L C S B E
G T Y T F T Y S A R S I P S S I Y Q E N H
U R O N L C T I E D R A O I M R C P S X E
I R P A N I T U M P J S D N V E R I F Y R
S G R H C D S G L P O O I D F X R J D L P
H O Q I W R P U K L E M U P J F Z E G E P
M Z L G U E C Q E S S D M R Z C V M L N A
Z E B P K V F C I R T N E C N O C H Y Y C
```

ACCOMPLICE	COUNSEL	INCIDENT	PREJUDICES
ACCUSATIONS	CULPRITS	INFER	PREMISES
ACQUAINTANCE	DEPRIVE	MENTOR	PROCEEDS
ADJOURN	DISMAY	MERELY	PURSUER
ADMISSIBLE	DISTINGUISH	MORAL	SALVATION
APPREHENDED	ELICIT	MOSAIC	SOLE
ASHY	EVIDENT	OBSCENE	SUICIDE
BOTCHED	GRACE	PAN	SUSTAINED
CACOPHONY	GROTESQUE	PAROLE	TRAUMA
CONCENTRIC	GRUESOME	PERPETRATOR	UNSHACKLE
CONSIGNING	GULLIBLE	PODIUM	VERDICT
CONTENTION	HESITATION	PRECIOUS	VERIFY
CORRIDOR	IMPEDE	PRECISE	VICIOUSLY

VOCABULARY WORD SEARCH ANSWER KEY Monster

ACCOMPLICE	COUNSEL	INCIDENT	PREJUDICES
ACCUSATIONS	CULPRITS	INFER	PREMISES
ACQUAINTANCE	DEPRIVE	MENTOR	PROCEEDS
ADJOURN	DISMAY	MERELY	PURSUER
ADMISSIBLE	DISTINGUISH	MORAL	SALVATION
APPREHENDED	ELICIT	MOSAIC	SOLE
ASHY	EVIDENT	OBSCENE	SUICIDE
BOTCHED	GRACE	PAN	SUSTAINED
CACOPHONY	GROTESQUE	PAROLE	TRAUMA
CONCENTRIC	GRUESOME	PERPETRATOR	UNSHACKLE
CONSIGNING	GULLIBLE	PODIUM	VERDICT
CONTENTION	HESITATION	PRECIOUS	VERIFY
CORRIDOR	IMPEDE	PRECISE	VICIOUSLY

VOCABULARY CROSSWORD Monster

Across
4. Attorney; one who gives advise
10. Mercy or good will of God
12. Money obtained from a venture
13. Hallway
14. Single
15. Only; simply
18. Pale; light-colored
19. Arising from the sense of right and wrong
22. The release of a prisoner before his term has expired
23. Complete loss of courage in the face of trouble
24. Can be allowed in
25. Intentionally killing oneself
26. Clearly expressed; distinct and correct in sound or statement

Down
1. Conclude from evidence
2. Keep from
3. Block; get in the way of
5. Vulgar; offensive; indecent
6. Slow, systematic camera movement to show a large view
7. Proceeding in a systematic order
8. People who plan an illegal or evil act
9. Trusted advisor or counselor
10. Bizarre; distorted; incongruous
11. Horrifying; shocking
15. Picture or design made up of small pieces
16. Jumbled, discordant sounds
17. Elevated platform for a speaker or conductor
20. Land and/or buildings
21. Bring forth

VOCABULARY CROSSWORD ANSWER KEY Monster

						1 I	2 D					
3 I				4 C	5 O	U	N	S	E	L	6 P	7 M
M		8 C	9 M		F		P	10 G	R	A	C	E	11 G
12 P	R	O	C	E	E	D	S	E		R	R	N	T	R
E		N		N		13 C	O	R	R	I	D	O	R	H	U
D		S		T		E				V		T	14 S	O	L	E
E		P		O		N		15 M	E	R	E	L	Y	D	S
		I		R		E		O			S			I	O
16 C		R				17 P		S			Q			C	M
A		18 A	S	H	Y	19 M	O	R	A	L		20 P	A	E
C		T				D		I				R	L
O		O		21 E		I		C				E	L
22 P	A	R	O	L	E		U			23 D	I	S	M	A	Y
H		S		I			M					I
O				C			24 A	D	M	I	S	S	I	B	L	E
N	25 S	U	I	C	I	D	E					E
Y			T			26 P	R	E	C	I	S	E

Across
4. Attorney; one who gives advise
10. Mercy or good will of God
12. Money obtained from a venture
13. Hallway
14. Single
15. Only; simply
18. Pale; light-colored
19. Arising from the sense of right and wrong
22. The release of a prisoner before his term has expired
23. Complete loss of courage in the face of trouble
24. Can be allowed in
25. Intentionally killing oneself
26. Clearly expressed; distinct and correct in sound or statement

Down
1. Conclude from evidence
2. Keep from
3. Block; get in the way of
5. Vulgar; offensive; indecent
6. Slow, systematic camera movement to show a large view
7. Proceeding in a systematic order
8. People who plan an illegal or evil act
9. Trusted advisor or counselor
10. Bizarre; distorted; incongruous
11. Horrifying; shocking
15. Picture or design made up of small pieces
16. Jumbled, discordant sounds
17. Elevated platform for a speaker or conductor
20. Land and/or buildings
21. Bring forth

VOCABULARY MATCHING 1 Monster

___ 1. CONSPIRATORS A. Money obtained from a venture
___ 2. MORAL B. Ruined through clumsiness
___ 3. MENTOR C. Slow, systematic camera movement to show a large view
___ 4. BOTCHED D. Horrifying; shocking
___ 5. PROCEEDS E. Helper in an illegal act
___ 6. ACCUSATIONS F. Hallway
___ 7. ADJOURN G. Clear; obvious; easily seen
___ 8. CULPRITS H. Holding back for reason of uncertainty
___ 9. CACOPHONY I. Deliverance from evil or difficulty
___ 10. EMPHATICALLY J. Boldly; definitely; accented
___ 11. EVIDENT K. Conclude from evidence
___ 12. SALVATION L. Caught
___ 13. PRECIOUS M. Suspend proceedings until another time
___ 14. TRANSCRIBED N. Written down
___ 15. HESITATION O. People who plan an illegal or evil act
___ 16. ACCOMPLICE P. Mercy or good will of God
___ 17. GRUESOME Q. Complete loss of courage in the face of trouble
___ 18. IMPLICATES R. Implies involvement
___ 19. CONDESCENDINGLY S. People guilty of a crime
___ 20. APPREHENDED T. Valuable
___ 21. DISMAY U. With an air of superiority
___ 22. INFER V. Arising from the sense of right and wrong
___ 23. CORRIDOR W. Trusted advisor or counselor
___ 24. PAN X. Charges of wrongdoings
___ 25. GRACE Y. Jumbled, discordant sounds

VOCABULARY MATCHING 1 ANSWER KEY Monster

O - 1.	CONSPIRATORS	A. Money obtained from a venture
V - 2.	MORAL	B. Ruined through clumsiness
W - 3.	MENTOR	C. Slow, systematic camera movement to show a large view
B - 4.	BOTCHED	D. Horrifying; shocking
A - 5.	PROCEEDS	E. Helper in an illegal act
X - 6.	ACCUSATIONS	F. Hallway
M - 7.	ADJOURN	G. Clear; obvious; easily seen
S - 8.	CULPRITS	H. Holding back for reason of uncertainty
Y - 9.	CACOPHONY	I. Deliverance from evil or difficulty
J - 10.	EMPHATICALLY	J. Boldly; definitely; accented
G - 11.	EVIDENT	K. Conclude from evidence
I - 12.	SALVATION	L. Caught
T - 13.	PRECIOUS	M. Suspend proceedings until another time
N - 14.	TRANSCRIBED	N. Written down
H - 15.	HESITATION	O. People who plan an illegal or evil act
E - 16.	ACCOMPLICE	P. Mercy or good will of God
D - 17.	GRUESOME	Q. Complete loss of courage in the face of trouble
R - 18.	IMPLICATES	R. Implies involvement
U - 19.	CONDESCENDINGLY	S. People guilty of a crime
L - 20.	APPREHENDED	T. Valuable
Q - 21.	DISMAY	U. With an air of superiority
K - 22.	INFER	V. Arising from the sense of right and wrong
F - 23.	CORRIDOR	W. Trusted advisor or counselor
C - 24.	PAN	X. Charges of wrongdoings
P - 25.	GRACE	Y. Jumbled, discordant sounds

VOCABULARY MATCHING 2 Monster

___ 1. PAN
___ 2. GROTESQUE
___ 3. COUNSEL
___ 4. CONTENTION
___ 5. PAROLE
___ 6. VICIOUSLY
___ 7. VERIFY
___ 8. GRUESOME
___ 9. PREJUDICES
___ 10. IMPLICATES
___ 11. ACCUSATIONS
___ 12. PERPETRATOR
___ 13. DISMAY
___ 14. CONCENTRIC
___ 15. MERELY
___ 16. UNSHACKLE
___ 17. ADJOURN
___ 18. ASHY
___ 19. SALVATION
___ 20. COMPASSION
___ 21. CONDESCENDINGLY
___ 22. DEPRIVE
___ 23. MENTOR
___ 24. ACCOMPLICE
___ 25. APPREHENDED

A. Point put forth in an argument
B. Suspend proceedings until another time
C. Keep from
D. Charges of wrongdoings
E. Slow, systematic camera movement to show a large view
F. Horrifying; shocking
G. Implies involvement
H. Prove the truth of
I. Bizarre; distorted; incongruous
J. Take off chains or restraints
K. Violently with mean or evil intent
L. Helper in an illegal act
M. The release of a prisoner before his term has expired
N. One who commits a crime
O. With an air of superiority
P. Causes an adverse judgement to be made before facts are considered
Q. Only; simply
R. Deliverance from evil or difficulty
S. Caught
T. Trusted advisor or counselor
U. Attorney; one who gives advise
V. Complete loss of courage in the face of trouble
W. Feeling or sharing the suffering of another in the intent of giving aid, support, or showing mercy
X. Having a common center
Y. Pale; light-colored

VOCABULARY MATCHING 2 ANSWER KEY Monster

E - 1.	PAN	A. Point put forth in an argument
I - 2.	GROTESQUE	B. Suspend proceedings until another time
U - 3.	COUNSEL	C. Keep from
A - 4.	CONTENTION	D. Charges of wrongdoings
M - 5.	PAROLE	E. Slow, systematic camera movement to show a large view
K - 6.	VICIOUSLY	F. Horrifying; shocking
H - 7.	VERIFY	G. Implies involvement
F - 8.	GRUESOME	H. Prove the truth of
P - 9.	PREJUDICES	I. Bizarre; distorted; incongruous
G -10.	IMPLICATES	J. Take off chains or restraints
D -11.	ACCUSATIONS	K. Violently with mean or evil intent
N -12.	PERPETRATOR	L. Helper in an illegal act
V -13.	DISMAY	M. The release of a prisoner before his term has expired
X -14.	CONCENTRIC	N. One who commits a crime
Q -15.	MERELY	O. With an air of superiority
J -16.	UNSHACKLE	P. Causes an adverse judgement to be made before facts are considered
B -17.	ADJOURN	Q. Only; simply
Y -18.	ASHY	R. Deliverance from evil or difficulty
R -19.	SALVATION	S. Caught
W 20.	COMPASSION	T. Trusted advisor or counselor
O -21.	CONDESCENDINGLY	U. Attorney; one who gives advise
C -22.	DEPRIVE	V. Complete loss of courage in the face of trouble
T -23.	MENTOR	W. Feeling or sharing the suffering of another in the intent of giving aid, support, or showing mercy
L -24.	ACCOMPLICE	X. Having a common center
S -25.	APPREHENDED	Y. Pale; light-colored

VOCABULARY JUGGLE LETTERS 1 Monster

1. SINNOGGINC = 1. _____
   Permanently handing over to

2. UDMPOI = 2. _____
   Elevated platform for a speaker or conductor

3. UIVCLSYIO = 3. _____
   Violently with mean or evil intent

4. IUPCSOER = 4. _____
   Valuable

5. ESOL = 5. _____
   Single

6. LCIITE = 6. _____
   Bring forth

7. UBYPLERAMS = 7. _____
   Reasonably assumed

8. SUPRITLC = 8. _____
   People guilty of a crime

9. HITGSSDIUNI = 9. _____
   Recognize apart from others

10. IFRVEY =10. _____
    Prove the truth of

11. TISEALPCIM =11. _____
    Implies involvement

12. ERHAPPDEDEN =12. _____
    Caught

13. RMTONE =13. _____
    Trusted advisor or counselor

14. DRCIVTE =14. _____
    Decision from a jury

VOCABULARY JUGGLE LETTERS 1 ANSWER KEY Monster

1. SINNOGGINC = 1. CONSIGNING
   Permanently handing over to

2. UDMPOI = 2. PODIUM
   Elevated platform for a speaker or conductor

3. UIVCLSYIO = 3. VICIOUSLY
   Violently with mean or evil intent

4. IUPCSOER = 4. PRECIOUS
   Valuable

5. ESOL = 5. SOLE
   Single

6. LCIITE = 6. ELICIT
   Bring forth

7. UBYPLERAMS = 7. PRESUMABLY
   Reasonably assumed

8. SUPRITLC = 8. CULPRITS
   People guilty of a crime

9. HITGSSDIUNI = 9. DISTINGUISH
   Recognize apart from others

10. IFRVEY =10. VERIFY
    Prove the truth of

11. TISEALPCIM =11. IMPLICATES
    Implies involvement

12. ERHAPPDEDEN =12. APPREHENDED
    Caught

13. RMTONE =13. MENTOR
    Trusted advisor or counselor

14. DRCIVTE =14. VERDICT
    Decision from a jury

VOCABULARY JUGGLE LETTERS 2 Monster

1. ORMAL = 1. _____
   Arising from the sense of right and wrong

2. BLEGIULL = 2. _____
   Easily deceived

3. GHIINTSSUDI = 3. _____
   Recognize apart from others

4. PEEDRIV = 4. _____
   Keep from

5. IPSRCLTU = 5. _____
   People guilty of a crime

6. TVOALIASN = 6. _____
   Deliverance from evil or difficulty

7. DISNAUTSE = 7. _____
   Upheld; supported; maintained

8. HDCBOET = 8. _____
   Ruined through clumsiness

9. EYVIRF = 9. _____
   Prove the truth of

10. CNUKLSEHA =10. _____
    Take off chains or restraints

11. RQGUEETOS =11. _____
    Bizarre; distorted; incongruous

12. TECNOCNICR =12. _____
    Having a common center

13. DSELNYINCEODNGC =13. _____
    With an air of superiority

14. IMOSCNPASO =14. _____
    Feeling or sharing the suffering of another in the intent of giving aid, support, or showing mercy

VOCABULARY JUGGLE LETTERS 2 ANSWER KEY Monster

1. ORMAL = 1. MORAL
   Arising from the sense of right and wrong

2. BLEGIULL = 2. GULLIBLE
   Easily deceived

3. GHIINTSSUDI = 3. DISTINGUISH
   Recognize apart from others

4. PEEDRIV = 4. DEPRIVE
   Keep from

5. IPSRCLTU = 5. CULPRITS
   People guilty of a crime

6. TVOALIASN = 6. SALVATION
   Deliverance from evil or difficulty

7. DISNAUTSE = 7. SUSTAINED
   Upheld; supported; maintained

8. HDCBOET = 8. BOTCHED
   Ruined through clumsiness

9. EYVIRF = 9. VERIFY
   Prove the truth of

10. CNUKLSEHA =10. UNSHACKLE
    Take off chains or restraints

11. RQGUEETOS =11. GROTESQUE
    Bizarre; distorted; incongruous

12. TECNOCNICR =12. CONCENTRIC
    Having a common center

13. DSELNYINCEODNGC =13. CONDESCENDINGLY
    With an air of superiority

14. IMOSCNPASO =14. COMPASSION
    Feeling or sharing the suffering of another in the intent of giving aid, support, or showing mercy

www.ingramcontent.com/pod-product-compliance
Lightning Source LLC
Chambersburg PA
CBHW051409070526
44584CB00023B/3346